BOUNCING BACK

BOUNCING BACK

Don McCalman's Story

as told to

John Brindley

First published in 2005 by Donjohn
© Copyright: Don McCalman
The moral right of the author has been asserted.
ISBN: 0 9551354 0 0

Contents

Foreword   vii

Introduction   xi

Chapter 1 – 'We All Go Through The Mill You Know'   1

Chapter 2 – Early Doors and A Love Too Far   12

Chapter 3 – Married Bliss and Times of Grief   21

Chapter 4 – A Shock 'Life' Sentence   30

Chapter 5 – Searching For Treasure   50

Chapter 6 – Heartbreak Hotel   62

Chapter 7 – Door To Door   96

Chapter 8 – A New Era Dawns   111

Chapter 9 – True Lust and True Love   125

Chapter 10 – No Messing   136

Chapter 11 – Fairytale and Myths   146

Chapter 12 – Dustbin of the World   153

Chapter 13 – The Battle I Can't Win   164

Chapter 14 – Sixty and Out   173

Appendix   187

Foreword by John Brindley

IT'S STRANGE how threads of very different lives sometimes come together...

As a local newspaper journalist since 1981, I have long been aware that I needed to write a book sooner rather than later.

It was never going to be about my own life, comparatively uneventful as that has been, but the idea of writing someone else's story has always appealed to me.

Don, on the other hand, found himself in the opposite situation.

As someone who has clearly 'lived', perhaps too much on some occasions, he also had a book inside him, but just needed that bit of help from a writer to help the dream to become reality.

When he came into our office at the Loughborough Echo, my then editor John Rippin asked me whether I would be interested in such a task.

A couple of weeks later I sat down with Don and I must admit it took me at least five minutes or so to say 'yes'.

Let's face it, if you know Don, he can be a very good talker and it can take that length of time to get a word in edgeways!

Seriously, though, I consider the task of writing this book to have been a privilege. I think the main reason for this is that here we are all, at last, being given a rare insight into the REAL Don McCalman.

That man has been kept hidden under the cloak of major responsibility, as he has patrolled the doors of Nottingham for more years than even he can care to remember.

He has also, perhaps, maintained a certain persona through the equally rigorous task of running his own businesses since the age of 21.

It has, as he explains in this book, often been far better that the real Don was unknown and he realises now that this has undoubtedly been to his own personal cost.

Throughout our time together Don has insisted that this is a 'warts and all' story. In other words it contains what really happened, rather than what he wished had occurred.

The other fascinating insight that I sincerely hope comes across in this work is that there is a very different side to Don than the image he has so earnestly presented.

Like that other self-appointed 'Sheriff of Nottingham', Brian Clough, who so sadly passed away as this book was being written, there is a disarming personal side to a man who, quite frankly, has scared many people stiff.

And, yes, some of his friends have also labelled Don 'the legend', in much the same way as Forest and Derby fans adored Cloughie.

I have no doubt that, to extend the comparison still further, that Don has served the city of Nottingham in a similarly praiseworthy way.

One of our better projects at the Loughborough Echo has been to award local New Year's Honours to those who truly deserve them.

Not those who by way of their position in life, riches and influence, could scarcely have failed to come to notice, but those who make a contribution to the community by their self-sacrificing actions.

Such people make the world a better, more human and, yes, a safer place... Such a man, I believe, is Don McCalman. As you discover in this book he has fearlessly put his own life on the line far more times than he can now recall.

If all the threats he has received actaully been carried, there would be no technology, modern or otherwise, with which to rebuild him.

Being a doorman, you appreciate, is a very thankless task – and, sadly, becoming increasingly more so by the day.

Speaking to a good friend of Don's, he revealed how difficult it was to persuade trained colleagues to go on the doors for about £40 a night when there had been four drive-by shootings on the preceding four Friday nights!

Don, however, wouldn't flinch at such a challenge. He has never shirked such onerous responsibilities in his professional life and would simply back himself to be too strong, too quick-thinking, or perhaps in this day and age, too lucky, to be second best to any low life.

But Don is very much of the 'old school' when it comes to door supervisors, to give them their correct present day term.

This work also charts the major changes that are taking place on the doors of pubs, night clubs and hotels today, both positive and, very probably, negative.

Whether they leave you and I, the general public, feeling more or less secure is a question I can only ask everyone to consider.

Finally, as I've hinted above, it has been my pleasure to get to know Don, the private man.

And what I have learned may well be a surprise to people who know him a great deal better than I ever will.

For this tough guy, who has put the fear of God into countless people, is also the same Don who kisses the photographs of his grandchildren each and every morning and whose eyes literally light up at the mere mention of his children.

He is, naturally enough, an enigma ... a unique mixture of darkness and light and philosophical enough in the later years of his life to appreciate the fact.

But then life has not been particularly kind to him.

For in his early forties, when he should have been settling down to enjoy his business and personal success, he found his life going in a completely opposite direction.

Please read on and come to your own conclusions about British justice before condemning too many others.

Yet, as the title of this book suggests, Don has come 'Bouncing Back', both literally on the doors and, I would suggest, as a human being.

I hope that in this book I have been able to introduce you to the real Don McCalman, truly one of Nottingham's great characters.

For all Don's self-confessed faults, a city, which I personally have a great regard for, would have been much the poorer for his absence.

Let Don's story begin.........

JOHN BRINDLEY

Introduction

ALL my life I've been a bit of a mystery, so much so that in later years, I've even earned the nickname of 'Howard Hughes'.

So why have I decided it is time now to lift the lid on my first 64 years and, so to speak, tell all?

Firstly, I think there is a right time...

When your friends have begun to nag away with 'When are you going to write a book?' and you have begun to run out of ready excuses, even the most stubborn soul knows the time is nigh.

Thanks therefore go to two of my best friends, Denis Thornhill and Dave Sankey, for continually reminding me that I needed to get on with it.

Both they and countless others have been a source of encouragement during the long months of preparing this book by telling me how much they were looking forward to seeing it.

It has helped me through the times when I honestly doubted it would ever happen.

In addition, I have found my life changing hugely during these last couple of years.

Life hasn't necessarily become any less hectic and certainly not any less complex, but I've come to be more reflective.

A man who has lived his life firmly in the fast lane, oblivious at times to many things I have passed by, has now started to appreciate what really matters. Relaxing with a cigar and looking out of the window of The Packe Arms at Hoton – one of my favourite haunts – I've begun to piece together some of the things I have done, both good and bad.

Bullied child, gang leader, husband, father, prisoner, head doorman, antiques, plumber and drains expert – I've been them all and more!

Yet, like the ultimate grumpy hospital patient, I have taken to older age two ways – badly and not at all. Being alone with my faithful dog Jason night after night in my security-conscious house, surrounded by many of the trappings of my business and personal life, is not proving an easy time for me.

Yes, I've got a lovely house and a Bentley car to die for, but what does it mean unless you have someone to share it all with?

I look at my photographs from my youth and my much less prized photos of today.

The Don of my youth was the centre of everyone's attention. I only had to walk into a room and I'd be surrounded by people.

Nowadays people glance when they see me driving around in my car, but they no longer see me.

The security that I've built around me has in a way become my personal prison.

This book, is my chance to break out of that self-imposed isolation for one last time.

I've started to think more about awkward subjects like death and the beyond and I wanted to leave a postscript not so much for the world, but for my grandchildren, my family as a whole, my friends and, not least, myself.

I have already begun to envisage reading these words on the patio of my home in Lenton, near Nottingham, with the odd tear in my eye, remembering all the good and not-so-good times and hoping that those who follow won't choose my own particular footsteps.

Every morning before I go out and about my business I kiss the photographs of my grandchildren – they mean so much to me.

Yet there's almost a tear in my eye when my beloved grandson, in his youthful naivety, declares: "When I grow up, I'd like to be like you."

Although, naturally enough, that fills me with pride, I would not wish upon my worst enemy – and I have a few! – the struggle and heartache that I've encountered along the way.

My life has been a constant gamble – I've won, lost, won and lost again and still can't be totally sure what the final verdict will be.

All I know is that I'm not the millionaire that some people presume me to be and I've worked harder than most could even dream of to get where I am today.

So I started thumbing through the Yellow Pages in search of an elusive ghost writer.

Not finding any such thing, I turned to my old friends at the Loughborough Echo, a newspaper I have advertised in for many years, and here it is.... my story.

I've enjoyed the last few months chatting to John, although there have been many days – a symptom of my illness perhaps – when I felt I'd rather scrap the idea and keep myself to myself.

If you allow me the privilege of summing it up, it's a tale of a schoolboy badly lacking in self confidence, who finds what he feels he wants in life – money, a good wife and family, house et al – then, just when he should have been in his prime, loses it all and more.

It's a story packed with incident and, as the title suggests, revolves a great deal around my almost life-long affair as a doorman.

It would have needed five books to detail all I've experienced on the doors of numerous hotels, pubs and clubs largely in the Midlands area.

But, after cringing so many times when watching TV depicting imaginary tough guys living pretend lives, it is definitely time I put a real-life example into print.

You see, I've been there, got the T-shirt of almost every scrape and challenging circumstance imaginable and lived to tell this tale. Just....

But there has been a double sting in the tail.

'Bouncing Back' means I have regained and rebuilt my finances, self respect and home a thousand times over in the last two decades.

Yet certain words from my now wife of 20 years Jackie have come to haunt me.

For, amid a life of affluence and style with a house and a Bentley car to die for and a series of successful businesses, I've discovered the cruelest truth of all.

You can have everything and yet in a very real way deep down have very little.

I realise now – and in all probability it is too late – that the image and presence I have created has helped to distance myself from what I really want. For by becoming the unknowable, the hard man of few words, I have contributed to fulfiling Jackie's prophecy that I would end up a lonely man. Reality has knocked on my door in a big way. The diabetes I have denied for several years has started to ravage me, taking from me the health I took for granted for so long.

I wish now that I had taken the condition more seriously when it was first diagnosed rather than just pushing it to the back of my mind and, in effect, hoping it would go away.

Yet I'd like to communicate with my loved ones to tell them more about the real Donald Stuart McCalman and leave them with an accurate, helpful and lasting memory.

I'd ask you, knowing that this is a true story, not to think too ill of me but to remember that we all make mistakes and, perhaps reading this, will help others in some way.

Also, if you allow me the self-indulgence, I'd like to speak about my concerns for Nottingham, the city I have lived in all my life, my country and my industry. I'm convinced that it is not just my age that recalls far safer, happier times when life was simpler, more family and community-orientated and had fewer of today's great worries.

Anyway, that's enough said for now. I hope you enjoy this read, appreciate it warts and all, and learn in some small way from it.

And to those to whom this book is truly dedicated – my family and my closest friends – I hope this is a way of remembering me when I finally go and meet my maker. Good reading.....

Chapter 1

'We All Go Through The Mill You Know'

AUGUST 3 1941 was the day I bounced into the world at our family home of number seven Bartholomew Road, in the St Ann's Well Road area of Nottingham.

All in all it was a normal enough welcome for Donald Stuart McCalman, a son for Agnes and Donald Alexander and a further male influence in a family otherwise dominated by females – my three sisters, Pat, Jean and Angela.

I was to be introduced into an 'average' family, neither wealthy, nor poor, but a happily close one. My father originated from New Zealand, with his passport revealing him to be of farming stock.

His parents were actually Scottish, so he was almost on home ground when he came to England to work and stayed at a boarding house in Drydon Street, Nottingham, run by Mrs Ashley, a close friend of my mother.

Dad was an electrician and also ran a bike shop. He was clearly more than a little impressed by what he saw of Nottingham folk, marrying Agnes at Shakespeare Street register office, and setting up home here. He was a big man, about 6' 3" tall and impressively broad. He worked hard to put food on our table and represented an obvious role model for a sometimes far from confident child.

The biggest influence of all on me in those early years was my mum.

In contrast to dad, she was a much smaller woman, about 5' 2" tall with brown eyes and probably a little overweight.

I say 'probably' because, to me, she was just mum and a fantastic woman in every way.

She was caring, kind and dedicated to the task of bringing up her family in times that the very small Don didn't recognise as being difficult.

Our semi-detached three-bedroom house was, for us, the perfect home in Bartholomew Road, Nottingham, on Donkey Hill, as locals know it.

Mention that part of Nottingham today and people simply shudder. Nearby St Ann's Well Road is virtually a no-go area and the murder of tragic 14-year-old Danielle Beccan walking home from the Goose Fair in October 2004 has only widened its fearsome reputation. Back then, it was a fantastic place to live, without any of the fears that must cross the minds of youngsters today.

Competing for attention from the seemingly endless terraced houses were a series of shops that I came to appreciate in their different ways.

There was Mrs Allen's, which used to sell bundles of wood to light our home fires. You could also get sweets, cigarettes, even bacon.

In addition I fondly recall the newsagent's, a dark shop attractive to me because of its wide range of tobacco, Masons the butcher's, a grocer's and Harry Bramley's, where in my early working days I loved getting a succulent pork chop and fresh tomato during my lunch hour.

And that's not to mention a good, old-fashioned fish and chip shop.

The house itself included wooden pillars to the front and leaded and French windows.

Other features included the marble floor in the hallway, a spiral staircase and the luxury of a toilet in the bathroom with a high-level cistern helping to contribute to a home that was a cut above the many depressing looking houses that characterised the nearby Meadows in war-torn Nottingham.

I say war-torn although, to be honest, I knew very little about why those strange sirens kept going off or why we as a family gathered not uncommonly in our cellar or even had a bunker in the garden.

Even the tell-tale presence of ration books in the years that followed had little or no real effect on my early existence.

For, whilst my mum ripped out coupons for a certain amount of tea, butter and meat or the like, we never seemed to go short and, anyway, there seemed a great joy in the simple things of life in those days. It might seem difficult for people now to think of life without computers, mobile phones and all the latest mind-boggling fashion assets and gadgets, but we possessed something else which, in my view, was far more precious.

There was a sense of community. Wealth we may not have even conceived of, but we were all together and supportive of one another – and not just because of the war.

There was a greater trust and openness about people, says he who now lives behind a barrier of trees and security cameras.

Happily enough, I always had my own space, the box room at the rear of the house.

This was basically the attic room, a sizable enough affair with a window in the roof offering a perfect view of Smart and Brown's, the furniture business, far below.

My resting place was a basic sprung plywood bed, with a chair next to it where the young McCalman would spend time eagerly devouring the weekly comics. I also soon enough adorned the room with plenty of pictures of motorbikes and still more of my idol, Elvis Presley.

There was an Indian painting, beautifully done by my art teacher and, more ominously perhaps, a gas mask from the war and a Canadian gun holster with a Colt 45 model enclosed.

I came along third in the family role of honour. Jean was the first born some eight years before me, Pat followed four years later and Angela is four years younger than I am.

We all got on well together. Jean and Pat were the brains behind the young family whilst Angela was probably not quite as strong as her two sisters, being instead a little more laid back and independent. There was quite a physical contrast, too, with Jean being petite, rather like my mum, Pat being much taller and Angela the slimmest.

I still recall those happy nights in front of the TV, a technological breakthrough in the McCalman household.

I would buy four bars of chocolate for just a couple of shillings and share them out whilst we watched the highly exciting invention they now call 'the box'.

Jean used to carefully wash her younger brother on the mangle and there were happy days going to the pictures as a family.

Dad encouraged an early love of gardening in me. I used to make paths around the apple tree in our back garden and grow my own spring onions and radishes. None of us used to worry too much about missing out on anything. Thank goodness there was no such thing as keeping up with the Joneses in those days.

Dad liked a pint, although he wasn't a drunkard or anything of the sort. I remember him giving me my first taste of beer when I was aged 12 from a barrel. "Have a taste of that lad," he said.

I must admit the real significance of such a momentous occasion slightly passed me by at the time.

After all, alcohol and working with people who are under its influence was to become a very major feature of my life.

Suffice to say that I thoroughly enjoyed it although not quite enough at that stage to get me hooked.

Many a night I remember waiting on the stairs for Dad to come back home. Not infrequently he'd come back in at about 10pm and settle down to a hot meal such as roast beef or chops.

It was worth staying awake because there was always the chance that we'd be invited down for a late-night treat.

It was the same much later when dad used to take me out and I'd maybe have a sip of beer and a packet of crisps.

You'd scarcely find a child excited at such a prospect these days, but somehow back then we appreciated things more and were definitely all the better for it. There was plenty of reason to feel secure.

I had respect for both my parents, a trait that sadly is less and less common and true of today.

Ours was a very strict upbringing and I'd no sooner have said a word out of place to either than volunteer for another beating at school.

It sickens me now to hear youngsters refer to their parents in the most derogatory terms in the street. You might hear one say 'that old bitch' about their mum or something equally rude and unflattering about their dad.

Really, they're the ones missing out if they think about the most important people in their young lives in that way.

As for me, I was far from a perfect son, but from a relatively early age, I would go crazy if anyone upset my mum.

There was to be one important moment when I wasn't there for her but, for now, that's a later story.

One of my highlights of the week was Sunday tea. My own particular main course was bacon and egg – I absolutely loved it – washed down by homemade lemonade and rice pudding.

And then there was Christmas, a real treat in the McCalman household.

Our own particular tradition was pork pie and pickled onions for Christmas breakfast.

We would get sacks full of sweets and presents that, although far more modest than today, were still very eagerly unwrapped.

I recall my excitement at tucking into some Buffalo Bill books and unveiling my own toy lorry.

Mum baked the most gorgeous Christmas cake imaginable, laced with rum and with a Santa in the middle. It was around two feet in diameter and seemed to last for ages, but none of us were complaining.

Then we settled down to a roast beef dinner, washed down by apple pie and cream, with some of our homemade lemonade for afters.

In my memory Christmas was so different back then. Even the climate seemed more appropriate.

I've always been one for the snow and the cold weather. I loved the echoes of crunching away in the snow.

Everything seems so much clearer and atmospheric than in the humid days of summer.

Those were the days, too, when the carol singers would come round and sing their hearts and souls out for a healthy time, rather than giving you a verse and then reaching their hands out.

I think also we appreciated looking forward to the festivities ourselves rather than being driven by commercialism to consider the first Noel as early as August or September.

New Year was a lovely family time too, as Dad, perhaps because of his Scottish roots, insisted we were all together on New Year's Eve.

We used to stay up to midnight and know the New Year was officially here when we heard the tones of Big Ben on the radio.

For all these comforts, life wasn't completely kind to the young Donald.

If anything, I was a nervous child, a trait well illustrated one day when there was a terrific thunderstorm.

The sight of water flooding down Donkey Hill with the speed of the Niagara Falls was just too much for the young McCalman and I just screamed and screamed my head off.

That was one of the first times that my parents were left to wonder just what they had taken on.

I didn't have high self-esteem and this was made still worse when I contracted pneumonia and bronchitis at the age of eight and had to wear unsightly leg irons for about three years.

This all started whilst I was at my first school, Walter Halls in Wells Road, and added hugely to what was a very depressing experience.

Nothing against Walter Halls, or nearby Morley Secondary, also in Wells Road, you'd understand, but I just didn't like school at all.

I never had any interest in academic subjects of any kind and I was very much a loner, setting a pattern that persists until this very day.

It will come as no surprise therefore to learn that I left school as early as I could at the age of 15 without taking any exams.

They say school days are the best of your life, but you can certainly count me out on that score. Wearing leg irons for three years, however, set me up for an experience that was far more serious and was also to have an effect far beyond the early ending of my studies.

As with countless poor people both before and since, being identifiable as a little different set me up as an obvious and easy target for the bullies – and that's just what happened.

The bullying involved about seven or eight people, some of them my age, others a little older. As most of you will recognise there are few more cowardly folk than bullies because they look for an obvious weakness and hammer away at the areas in which they can hurt you.

Having had pneumonia and whooping cough, that had left problems with my legs, I found it hard to run and they exploited my distress.

They'd tease me by giving me a small amount of time to try to get away before rounding on me.

There's no doubt in my mind that my experiences left mental scars. Bullying always does.

Although I had friends such as Mick Smith, Denis Leavey, Brian Boot, Sam Lander, Bernard Glagden and Malcolm Smith, it probably did have an influence on my ability to mix.

When you're in that sort of fix, it's on your mind all the time and it has unfortunate side effects in other areas of your life.

Sometimes I'd walk miles out of my way just to avoid the lads.

My memories of that time are a little hazy, but the bullying was physical as well as mental.

I remember some lads standing me in some water, knowing that I just couldn't get away, and taunting me.

They used to take the mickey out of me and it really hurt.

You might tell your children that the answer is to confide in someone, but it is rarely as simply as that.

Certainly I never told my teachers at school, as this was the obvious route to more concerted beatings.

And the only occasions when my parents found out were when it got to such an extreme they could barely fail to notice.

To be brutally honest, I wasn't very good in any case at sharing my feelings and thought I needed to fight my own battles.

The bullying was to have other, more lasting, repercussions too.

I've no doubt that it contributed to a childhood fear of confined spaces that led to my having to attend a clinic in Chaucer Street, near the arboretum.

I went there a good many times, but it never came near to solving the problem.

Instead that happened through a much more radical form of 'therapy' in my forties.

Another legacy of my childhood was a fear of going to sleep.

I can't recall whether this was linked with the fact that my mum took me downstairs to sleep whilst I was in my leg irons, but certainly it lived with me. It has always made me fearful of operations. So far, luckily enough, I've had just one for a hernia after some over-stressful lifting.

The doctors in hospital assured me I was never actually put to sleep, although I suspect that I must have been. I think it's all to do with a fear of losing control.

Dad kindly indulged my liking for target shooting by buying me a bow and arrow. But, again, the bullies soon managed to take away my joy.

I was grateful to Dad for going to school to find the lads who did it even though my pride told me even then that it should have been my job.

Mum and Dad didn't go out a lot together, although I recall them going to a pub called The Westminster about once a week. But they were undoubtedly close as later sad events were to most poignantly underline. Arguments were sorted out quickly and efficiently, even other people's.

I remember most vividly the impressive way in which Dad dealt with a row between a neighbour, a plasterer called Mr Price, and another man.

He picked them up by the collar and merely cleared them off – a fine lesson indeed for the doorman-to-be. Then, suddenly, the boy whose battles had been largely fought for him by his loyal mum and dad turned. The unwitting recipient was a lad who was always showing me up in front of my mates.

Don't ask me why or how it happened but this time I just waded in and hit him.

I can still see him now roaring like a baby as I repeated the dose several times over.

For once in my life it made me feel ten foot tall and certainly had a strong psychological affect on me from then on.

Almost from that point forward, I have always been one to stick up for myself.

I subsequently got involved in a few more punch-ups at school and came off none the worse.

It was strange but the boy who was always being bullied was being transformed into the gang leader, the boss, that I've always been ever since.

Looking back, I'm convinced now that it was actually because of my bullying past that I've always had to be 'top dog'.

I'd also learnt the invaluable life-lesson that everything changes the moment you stand up to people. Let the bullies rule the roost and they'll continue to exploit you and make things difficult, but once you've made it clear that you are strong enough to stand your ground it's amazing how quickly they back off.

Cowards, absolute cowards...

Naturally we got up to a fair deal of mischief but when I talk about gangs you're more than likely to get the wrong end of the stick.

There was scarcely any such thing then as stabbings or shootings. That is a part of modern-day Nottingham that was happily unknown in the 1950s.

I remember the complete shock of hearing about a murder when a young girl was set upon by a lad who took her up Union Road and battered her to death over the head with a brick.

Such events were almost unheard of in those days. You'd hardly ever hear about a rape or a particularly violent assault, so a murder shook us all up even more. Perhaps that was a sign of the times to come.

Our lifeblood was more naughty pranks.

Once, I recall our bid to fairly innocently get up the noses of neighbours through a door-knocking stunt that backfired.

I ended up producing one of the slowest and most unconvincing get-aways of all time as I combined running with compulsive laughter.

Later I rightly earned the wrath of my dad when I was caught scrumping and was taken to the police station. At that time the very disgrace of being caught by the police and, still worse, waiting for my dad to arrive was enough to keep me on the straight and narrow.

The police carried with them a respect and awe then that is again not so easy to maintain in politically correct times.

There was no way I wanted to get on the wrong side of them.

Yes, my dad gave me a good smacking, but not in an unduly violent way.

Many lads now would expect their parents to take their side against the authorities even when they'd committed such a 'crime'.

But I know which approach is healthier as far as I'm concerned.

Another main theme on my mind was to look as much like Elvis as possible.

My friends and I just loved The King and that made Ted Bullock, the hairdresser in St Ann's Well Road, an important man to know.

He knew just how to Brylcreem my hair and reproduce those famous sideburns.

He also used to sell 'Johnny bags' if we proved too irresistible with the young ladies.

Some chance!

At the age of 15 I landed my first job, filling banana boxes on Sneinton Market.

It may not have been the most fulfilling of vocations, but it was a start and earned me £6 and ten shillings per week.

And it was there that, for the first time, I started to notice something else that naturally enough was going to play an important role in my life – the opposite sex.

Seeing the young girls strolling through the market was consolation enough for the hours when bananas were the limit of my excitement.

My curiosity was aroused as I watched them chatting in their twos and threes or walking alone, presumably on their way home.

They represented something exciting, yet unobtainable, in a way that is not always the case nowadays.

You must appreciate that, up to that point, I'd scarcely landed a smacker on a girl's lips, let alone really 'scored' with a bird.

That's not to say, of course, that among mates I hadn't exaggerated any minor success I might have had for my own entertainment and social standing. Anyhow, I was soon to be making up for any lost time!

Looking back on those topsy-turvy days, I will always remember words from my dear mum one night that seemed innocuous enough at the time.

There she was walking me home from The Cavendish cinema when she turned and said: "We all go through the mill you know, we're bound to go."

They were words that were very familiar to me as she often used to sing them out loud.

Like so many people, I would view my childhood as a struggle as much as a pleasure – but one that somehow had to be undertaken before the next chapters of my life could be written...

Chapter 2

Early Doors and A Love Too Far

EVERYONE, I suspect, who gets involved with an activity that is to play a huge role in their lives can recall early role models.

The first doorman that I can actually remember was a Mr Rains, who was based at The Cavendish cinema on St Ann's Well Road. I became a regular visitor there in my teens, recalling watching such classics as Love Me Tender starring the inimitable Elvis and a string of timeless Westerns.

Costing just a shilling to view the downstairs screen and one and six to go upstairs, it was great entertainment and a more than welcome distraction from the routine of working with bananas.

Mr Rains – we never made it onto first name terms, you understand – was a suitably impressive-looking man with a military air about him. With his hair combed straight back and his smart looks, he always gave the impression of being both fit and alert to every little thing that was going on.

My strongest memory of him came when, unsurprisingly perhaps, I got on the wrong side of him due to my own way of sorting out cinema problems.

I was with my friend Mick Smith watching a film when I got involved in an argument with this bloke in front of me, who was probably about 10 or 11 years older. In my mind, he was making far too much noise so I leant forward and gave him a smack on the head. Unfortunately, his screams then brought the whole cinema to a halt, the lights went up and there was Mr Rains ushering us to the front.

But, before we could sort things out, the man tried to exact his revenge by having a go at me, so I hit him again and this time he fell on top of a woman.

Mr Rains took us to the area near the kiosk and asked us both what was going on. In the end he put me on a warning about my future behaviour and, after threatening to kick the other bloke out, settled for ensuring we sat nowhere near each other for the remainder of the film.

Needless to say my behaviour wasn't exactly saintly at The Cavendish from that moment on, but I emerged with a healthy respect for how Mr Rains had done his job.

The man who influenced me most at that time, however, and also gave me my first real break on the doors was Johnny Rice.

Based at the Empress Cinema about 10 minutes walk from The Cavendish at the end of St Ann's Well Road, Johnny was destined to impress me from the very start. His CV included working for some of the biggest names in London and he personally knew the Kray twins, whom I've always had a good regard for. One incident that stuck in my mind was the sight of this big man with a distinctive scar on his face clambering over the cinema seats to get to these lads who were causing a disturbance,

Once outside, he followed up with a thumping uppercut which took one young man clean over the rails.

Johnny was a tough guy, pure and simple. People looked up at him then in much the same way as they were to regard me when I was in my prime.

I told him I'd like to do what he did and he replied: "All right, I sort out the trouble, you pull the ladies. Not a bad deal I thought for a tall, dark and broad youth with jet-black hair who was just beginning to become aware of the fairer sex.

After working for three or four weekends – I was on the door on both Friday and Saturday nights – I got involved in my first real fight.

Still being rather naive as a doorman, I emerged both blackened and cut. Physically battered I might have been, but, more importantly, my ego was well massaged when a friend, Brian Barnaby, came round to our house and told my mum that if it hadn't been for my bravery he would have been kicked to hell.

Johnny and I used to have the odd drink together socially and I soon got another close-up example of his style. We'd been to the Admiral

Duncan for a jar or two and words had been exchanged between Johnny and a couple of lads in the pub.

As we were walking back up St Ann's Well Road, three blokes coming up behind us started calling Johnny again.

He swung round and I saw his hand come out and knock the first guy to the floor, before he kicked number two in his private parts and sent the other thudding into a shop window where he lay with both feet out on the deck.

There were still people around wondering what was going on, so we legged it as quickly as we could. I didn't make such a good job of it as my legs were fairly stiff from all the tension, but Johnny was still laughing as we made our escape.

We stayed over at his mum's house that night and I couldn't sleep. I couldn't help wondering whether we'd wake up and find out that the bloke had been killed. In the event there was nothing but the boarded up shop window to remind us of the incident.

Johnny was the ultimate professional at all times, a trait well illustrated for my eyes one afternoon.

We'd gone to Victoria Park, which was close to the old Empress, because there was still some time before we were due to start work.

Johnny fell asleep in the park, using his jacket as an impromptu pillow. As time was fast approaching for our shift, I went up to him and said: "Johnny!" Immediately he was bolt upright and ready, it seemed, to knock the living daylights out of me. And, in no time at all, he was in and out of the cinema toilets, brushed up and looking as fresh as a daisy.

Meanwhile my personal confidence took a massive lift when, away from running the doors, I caught up with an old school 'pal' and exacted some long overdue revenge.

This lad had been one of the group of school bullies who had made my life a misery when I was trapped in the leg irons. They'd made me stand in water, then run for my life towards some railings with the group in hot pursuit.

It was a good few years later, as you can imagine, but his image was still fresh enough in my mind for me to recognise him in a pub one Saturday evening. "Remember me, you bastard!" I said, grabbing him and dragging him outside. I hit him and hit him hard, jumping on his arm for good measure. He was someone I had absolutely no qualms about hurting. Bullies are the lowest of the low.

I was getting this rush of adrenalin that's still there whether you're a first-timer or an old-stage doorman and the gratifying feeling that I knew I could do this.

My parents, however, still needed a little more convincing.

"I'm just grateful I haven't got any more sons like you," said mum after I came home from a particularly torrid night.

I'd been to The Rose in Parliament Street, near to The Royal Hotel. At that time the pub was one of the more notorious in the city for trouble, but I hadn't been looking for any as I'd just been out with Johnny Rice for a drink.

The trouble started after Johnny had left to see his girlfriend. Somehow I got involved in a fight inside the pub and these lads vowed at the end of it that they'd get their revenge.

Unfortunately it happened a lot quicker than I'd anticipated.

I had just walked past this gateway on the way home when someone grabbed me round the neck and started punching me in the face. It felt like he was using a knuckle duster.

My face was scarred and I think I was knocked unconscious. Next thing I knew I was kneeling over a bin, with blood pouring from both sides of my face. I felt very wobbly and could not remember where I was. My back was also badly bruised and my shirt and jacket had both been ripped.

I got into a taxi and the driver offered to take me to hospital. I declined, but asked that he took me back home to Bartholomew Road instead. When I got up at about 11am I ached all over and must have looked a right mess.

My mum wondered what on earth had happened to me and I wasn't able to enlighten her a whole lot.

Fortunately for her, perhaps, there were soon to be other things on my young mind.

I met my first real girlfriend in a hotel on Mansfield Road. We started chatting, going out for drinks and, soon enough, a fair bit more. Up to that point I'd been restricted to just kissing and fumbling, but this was the real thing.

One night we were back at her parents' house and couldn't wait to get each other's clothes off. Talks about the birds and the bees don't really come into it at that stage and I found no difficulty in doing what came naturally. She was dark, tall and had a good body, all of which helped to keep me well exercised for a good three months.

Then, when things had quietened down, another girl walked into my life. Her name was Sandra Baverstock. She was sweet sixteen, I was just two years older. She was blonde, slim and had a good figure.

It doesn't take a detective to work out why she became my first wife. The fact of the matter was it was largely down to that most urgent of human drives – sex.

We had met when I used to go down to Le Carno. I'd be with Brian Barnaby, Mick Smith and some of my other mates and Sandra was with her mates.

At first I fancied her friend, Hazel Brierley, who lived on Cavendish Road, near Sandra. But, soon enough, it was Sandra I became involved with as we enjoyed nights out at the likes of Le Carno, the Empress Cinema and the Cavendish.

Needless to say the inevitable happened and within six months Sandra was pregnant.

I told my mum – that bit was ok- but when her father found out he was furious. Mostly, it has to be said, with me. To be honest he went a bit wild, yet didn't seem too upset with his own daughter for some reason.

At least he went short of trying to land one on me. Good job really because I would have laid him out good and proper!

Sandra was the one who was keen to get married whilst, to me, the idea of every night in bed with her was a strong pulling point. We were very strongly physically attracted to each other. I'd liked nothing more than coming home from work at lunchtime to have sex with her.

I was working at the Gas Board at the time and remember trudging to work carrying my tools with me in a bag over my shoulder, already thinking about what I'd be doing later in the day.

Sandra's mum was very keen on me getting a better job – my mind was 'on the job' but not the job she was thinking of!

Mum came to the wedding which was held at Bulwell Register Office in Highbury Vale. Sandra wore a pink suit with a short skirt and sported a hat fit for Ascot itself. I was dressed in a suit. Smart enough for the occasion, not that it meant that much to me.

I can't say that at the time I greatly believed in marriage and my thoughts are no more generous towards that grand institution today for that matter.

The words are pretty meaningless when you think about it. There has been too much water under the bridge in my life – and countless other lives too – to really believe in the sanctity of marriage.

It all adds up to what you get at the end of the day – a piece of paper! And, even then, you can get opt out clauses put in the deal these days.

There was nothing else that was too exotic about the occasion. We did not have a car, so we went home on the bus and never really considered the issue of a honeymoon.

There were much more pressing matters to consider – after all, Sandra was already heavily pregnant with Richard the first of our two sons. John was to follow about a year later.

Initially, at least we had the problem of living with her parents in Mapperley. More obvious still when you consider that Sandra's mother was against our alliance from its very beginnings.

I was just 18 years old when our first child was born – far too young. I didn't take too kindly to all this sudden added responsibility and it didn't help having the mother-in-law shaking her fist at me and living, as we did, in a strange house.

We moved to our own house in Gordon Road when Sandra got pregnant again, but it quickly became obvious that she was far from settled there.

Our social life wasn't quite what I was used to. We went to play bingo with Sandra's mum and one of her friends. Her mum used to take pleasure in telling me how well I'd done to become one of her family. But when I looked at her I was never that convinced! Let's put it this way – it was a mystery where Sandra had got her good looks from!

Sandra and her mum were extremely close which added to our tensions. Altogether our marriage barely lasted 18 months and, to be honest, I'd rather not stretch my brain cells too much and try to recall too much of it.

In truth, this time of my life never meant that much to me.

Sandra was, in retrospect, a stepping stone in my life. An exciting, alluring and sexual one admittedly when our passion was at its height but when that faded there was all too little left.

It didn't help that we lived in a dreadful old terraced house complete with outside toilet. The rent was about £1 and ten shillings a week and that was too much for that old dump.

Sandra's mum took great delight in reminding us at frequent intervals that she lived in a much better house in a much nicer area. Good for her.

When the split came it was quite sudden – and permanent.

We had got a house on Gordon Road and Sandra was now expecting John. She came home one Friday evening and delivered the bombshell: "My mum wants us to go back and live with her again." Instead of fighting my corner, I said: "You do it". When I came home from work the following lunchtime she had gone. I did the natural thing and went to the pub. Needless to say I got very drunk that day.

Her mother knocked at the door to claim Sandra's things. I was in no mood to resist. We lived apart for a while. I went back to my parents and Sandra lived with hers.

Ending things altogether wasn't quite so easy in those days. We met a couple of times on Wells Road and made some attempt to get back together, although by that time the attraction of the single life was a greater pull than being tied down with a family.

I wasn't going to get out of it that easily of course.

Those were the days when marriage was taken very seriously, particularly by the courts.

We talked with court officials trying to get us back together. That probably played a part in us meeting on a few further occasions, but there was never going to be much prospect of glueing together the practically unstickable.

There are times in your life when you probably know you are straying off the path that destiny has laid out for you, yet for some reason you go ahead and do it anyway.

Sandra Baverstock, nice girl though she was, was never going to be the love of my life and, for that reason alone, we were probably doomed from the beginning.

The hard realities of marital failure may not have hit me in the heart at that stage – I was soon out and about chasing most things I could find in a skirt – but they did hit me in the pocket.

The court ordered me to pay £3 and ten shillings per week for the maintenance of my two sons, serious enough money in those days.

The other painful truth was that I lost contact with my children – another effect perhaps of the original cause of getting married too young and too soon.

I visited them for a short while, but Sandra's mum made it more and more difficult for me to see them.

Looking back obviously there is hurt there, but it is difficult to miss what you never really had.

You only really get to know people by living with them and I never really got that chance.

But there's no way now I can play Dad when I've hardly ever seen them. It was a shock to my system when recalling this part of my life to reflect that, as far as I know, John is now 45 years old and Richard is 47. It barely seems possible.

I've seen very little of Sandra either. Some time later she came up to me in Parliament Street and gave me back a gold chain that I'd bought for her. I casually tossed it over the railway line and she was in tears. She had got to know something about me because she asked me why I was getting married again.

The last time I saw her was a good few years after that when she saw me working as a doorman at The Royal. She came up to me and said with an ironic twist to her voice: "This job probably suits you!" She was right – it suited me a great deal more than she did, poor girl.

Looking back now naturally I have some regrets. I can appreciate, in retrospect, how hard it must have been for her to bring up two sons

– my sons at that – on her own. It isn't an easy task for anyone and I've plenty of sympathy now for anyone left in that situation.

I'd noted that she had taken to motherhood very naturally and well, but that might be my memory trying to rid me of some of the guilt. Also, in retrospect, I realise now that Sandra needed her own mother at that time in her life because she, too, perhaps was too young to deal with everything on her own.

The truth is that I'd barely begun my life and the idea of being trapped for the rest of my days didn't really appeal to me.

It's strange, isn't it, that when you form an important relationship you lose something as well as gain – and that was my independence.

My adventures with the opposite sex were just about to begin rather than end....

Chapter 3

Married Bliss and Times of Grief

I DOCUMENT some of my exploits between my two marriages elsewhere. They were largely crazy, boozy and inconsequential with plenty of laughs and fallings out along the way.

One incident just about sums the whole strange time up.

I used to go to the pub with a lad called Alan, who lived in St Ann's Well Road. One day he said he knew of a flat where there were a couple of young women who wouldn't mind seeing us.

As it happened, the dice were loaded in his favour. There he was having sex with the girl he fancied upstairs whilst I was left with her friend. I wouldn't say she was bad looking at all, but there was really nothing between us and I didn't appreciate her sitting on my knee and telling me: "I love you!" In fact for once I was spending most of my time fighting her off.

It was actually quite a relief for me when Alan's bird suddenly shrieked that her husband was approaching the house. I took the chance to make a nifty getaway, clambering out of a window, over a fence and into the road where we'd left our Vauxhall Estate.

That's when the fun started. I spent the next 10 minutes wondering what was happening to my mate. Had the husband murdered him? Or what state would he be coming back out in?

I couldn't believe my eyes, however, when I actually saw him. He had the most angry look on his face, but was pushing a pram up the road towards the car.

Then he tried desperately to fold up the pram in the boot whilst I tried to find out what had gone on. Surely he wasn't that fast a mover!

"No," he explained. "When her husband asked her what on earth I was doing there, she answered that I'd come about the pram they'd advertised for sale in the paper!"

"Well, he bloody well better buy it then," said the husband and poor Alan had dug out a fiver from his pocket and made his most unusual of escapes.

We chucked the pram on some wasteland on the way back home, but it was worth far more than a fiver in entertainment value when we re-told the story time and again.

Generally I used to meet women in town, going round the pubs and enjoying myself. I found I met lots of women, but none made anything like the same impression on me as the lady who came next.

It was three years after the end of my first marriage – and many a fairly inconsequential fling later – that my eyes set sight on Jackie Warren for the very first time.

I used to watch her walking on Abbey Bridge long before she was aware of me. Now, I know that love is blind, but Jackie was a stunner. Lovely hair, a gorgeous figure to die for and the ability to dress up and really look the part.

I told my friend Bobby Coyne that this lovely woman, whom I saw wearing a distinctive red coat would soon be mine.

But the crunch moment came when I made my move. I got this phone call from a woman saying she was Jackie and seeing whether I was interested in going out for a date. It didn't take me too long to answer, even though the person on the other end of the phone was actually Jackie's mate!

Still we soon met for real. I picked her up at a bus stop, went to the pictures and for a drink – finding out that Jackie enjoyed a bottle of VP wine for a bit of Dutch courage – and what I had imagined for so long was beginning to come true.

I was working for myself as a gas fitter and plumber at the time and could soon juggle my workload to ensure I saw plenty of this new conquest.

There were some things to remind me of the Sandra experience.

Firstly, her father took an instant dislike to me. He'd rather look through the window than talk to me eye-to-eye and made no secret of the fact that he was unhappy that I had been previously married,

During those early months he even went to the extent of encouraging Jackie in any other potential friendship that came her way.

Ironic really that as a barman at The George Hotel, where I was to work later on the doors, he did actually have something in common with me.

We got on famously as time developed and he'd run me a bath to welcome me back home after a strenuous day.

The other common thread was that Jackie fell pregnant with our son Darryl. This time it was me who took the plunge and asked Jackie to marry me although she wasn't quite so sure. I spoke to her mother one night and she explained Jackie's fear that, after being married once already, I might not settle down properly.

Anyway, she soon came round and another wedding was arranged. But first there was a third person to consider.

My son was born at home just before the wedding. I was at my parents' house at the time when Jackie's mum made an urgent phone call. I drove like a madman to try to get there in time, but was still too late. I've never been present at the birth of any of my children.

To be honest, I've never felt a tinge of guilt or regret about that. I know the modern day idea is for the husband or boyfriend to be present, but in my mind it's an intensely private experience for the mother and not something I wanted to see. You can understand then that on this occasion I was actually quite relieved to discover I was late.

The wedding in a register office in Shakespeare Street was once again a quiet affair, although this time it meant a lot more to me. Jackie looked lovely, although my mind was already turning towards the night ahead!

Then Jackie, her parents and I went for a celebration meal to a place near Long Eaton.

I say her parents because mine weren't present. I had told my mum the date we were getting married but had not invited her. So when we walked into her shop, Yates', a wine lodge in Market Street, and told her how it had gone you can imagine it was a strange occasion.

Don't ask me why I treated her in this way. I still don't really know even to this day. Jackie's mum told me I should have invited her and naturally she was right.

It seems somehow that however much we love our nearest and dearest we still fail to treat them properly on some occasions and this was one of those occasions. It just happened to be a pretty major one!

I could tell that she was upset afterwards and I felt really awful about it all. I still do.

It wasn't that she didn't get on with Jackie. She most certainly did. The reasons for my error of judgment must lie deeper within myself. Perhaps the truth is that because this was my second wedding I was concerned about what she really thought about it.

This time we did actually have a honeymoon, a one-night affair in The Grand Hotel in Leicester, and we settled down happily to life as a family.

Those first few years of married life with Jackie were probably the happiest period of my entire life. Soon enough we had another addition to the family, our daughter Lisa, and I was quite a hands-on sort of father this time around.

I gladly took my turn to get up in the middle of the night and attend to the crying kids. Perhaps it was a sign that I was happy and they were just an extension of my new-found joy.

We lived at number 17 Lois Avenue, next door to her parents. Yet there were no similar problems as in my first marriage. I got on well with both her parents and they didn't restrict me from keeping in touch with my own.

There are all sorts of little things you do as a family that probably don't make the greatest of reading, but mean a lot to you at the time. We were well pleased with our new kind of life and just wished it could have stayed that way.

We used to meet up at dinner time during the week and drop into a small shop where we bought a cob and a tin of soup. Then we'd go back to my mum's where I'd add curry powder to the soup for lunch. Cosy, simple and yet so lovely.

Destiny, however, rarely throws you a bed of roses without a lot of thorns and stinging nettles to accompany them and so it was that problems outside our immediate family started to choke our lives some four years into our marriage.

At first there was a near miss that made me into a mini local hero. One morning there was a fire next door and our curtains were caught by the blaze. It was about 8am and I grabbed our two young children, Lisa and Darryl, and pulled them to safety. The local Nottingham Evening Post newspaper made a big feature of it saying that a father had saved his children from a fire. I think Jackie still has the cutting.

Next, however, came a series of unfortunate events from which there was to be no escape.

I could see my mum getting tired. She had always been a very hard worker, but gradually wasn't quite the same woman I'd always known and loved.

By the time she started complaining about headaches and went to see her optician, we all suspected that there was more to this than met the eye. The cautious comments of the optician only added to my fears.

She went to the doctors a couple of times and I know there were concerns about the possibility of a stroke or a blood clot. Three of her relatives had already died from strokes and I think the headaches were a warning sign. Mum's eyes were also beginning to look a little blood shot.

Anyway I was driving over Trent Bridge one night with my work mate Mick Alvey when I suggested we go and see my mum. The journey would have taken no more than 10 or 15 minutes and Mick had no problem with the idea.

Why we didn't go, I still can't really explain to this day. And I still regret it.

The very next morning I got an awful phone call from my sister Pat. My mum had passed away of a suspected stroke, aged 57. It was one of those life-changing moments that were to affect me for the rest of my days.

I went to see her, along with my dad and my three sisters, to pay my respects at Nottingham General Hospital. Looking at her lying in the coffin, it was as though she wasn't there at all. It wasn't the woman I remembered. I remember touching her for the very last time and filling up with tears.

It was an awful time. I suddenly felt dizzy and sick and my sister, Pat, had to steady me on the stairs. I started to mentally torture myself for not choosing to visit her that last night and for not inviting her to the wedding. I couldn't get over her death for months and months and, in a sense, I'm sure I never have.

It was a hammer blow that was difficult to come to terms with and, at first, caused some angst with Jackie.

On that very morning, she went out shopping with her sister.

I didn't like the fact that for her, at least, life was going on, although in retrospect I can look back now and understand her in a way.

The truth was that Jackie just wasn't able to take on board what had happened, something I know that has been true of me many times since.

It got no easier at the funeral when I was shocked that one of my aunties didn't seem to want to know me. She chose that moment to tell me that I'd been nothing but trouble to my mum and I honestly could have smacked her.

But, in truth, she was absolutely right. My mother had never stopped giving to me, yet I'd chosen to repay her by causing her the aggravation of having to cope with my fights, continually getting into scrapes and more recently the worries over children and my two marriages.

I have had some strange experiences in my life that have strengthened my belief that the dead are still somehow with us.

I recall not long after my mum passed away having a very strong feeling that she was at the bottom of the bed and was trying to communicate to me the fact that she was all right and I need worry no more about missing her that notable night.

There was nothing, however, that could give my father any such comfort. The sudden loss certainly had a dreadful effect on my poor old Dad. For the next few months we literally watched him go further and further downhill.

He was a broken man after losing his life partner. Each and every Sunday he would have lunch at our house and then the two of us would walk up to Redhill Cemetery to pay our further respects.

But, by the week, the once fine figure of a man was fading before my very eyes.

He was working during those months as a salesman to try to bring in some money, enough to go out for a few drinks at night.

But each evening would end with a sobbing Dad on the telephone pouring his heart out over how much he missed my mum. It was difficult to listen to him like this, but there was little more I could do.

One day when I went round to his house, he was clearly unwell and I had him taken to Nottingham City Hospital suffering from heart trouble.

He was given electric shock treatment, but wasn't really in a mood for a fight.

I left him one Sunday at 4pm and had a phone call from the doctor about 6.30pm.

My wife Jackie answered the inevitable call – my father had died, he said, literally from a broken heart. It was 10 months to the day since my mum had died.

What can't be taken away though is that such losses have a very profound effect on a young person.

Two such emotional losses were enough to have had a very profound effect on me. They say, however, that bad things come in threes and that's exactly what happened to me.

Mick Alvey was a tough lad, who lived life in the fast lane and made a fair few enemies. He'd not had an easy time during his 30 years, his mum died very early and his dad suffered from an alcohol problem.

I worked with him for a couple of years and we had some fantastic days together. I remember driving around town with him in my Ford Zephyr, listening to the music of the Rolling Stones and watching the girls go by. Two smart-looking lads in a smart car, we thought the world was our oyster, but not for long.

Around this time he'd been selling chocolate to make a bit of pre-Christmas money, but he wouldn't be seeing the festive season himself.

One Saturday afternoon I went round to his house in Nottingham Road, Basford, and he was in an unusually pensive mood. He was sitting on the settee, with his girlfriend looking on, and I just asked him what was wrong. "I haven't a clue what it is," he replied. "I've just got this funny feeling that something is going to happen." I said goodbye that day, not knowing it would be for the very last time.

Next day I was driving along when I heard some dreadful news on Radio Nottingham. "Michael John Alvey has been killed in a car crash," said the broadcaster. "His car hit a tree."

He had died how he lived – in a hurry. For some reason his car had hit a tree in Clifton, not far from where we run a door now. No other car was involved and his girlfriend was injured.

To see him laid out in the funeral parlour was such a shock to my system. It was certainly a bit too much for my mate Terry Bloomfield who collapsed at the sight of such a big, strong man laid low. So there I was with Mick with his arms across his chest in the coffin and my mate Terry spreadeagled on the floor. What a world!

I had looked death in the face in such a personal and traumatic way three times in less than two years. Never before nor since have I been touched in such a way, as the other deaths that have really affected me have been the losses of the likes of Princess Diana, whom I talk about later in this book, the great, lamented Elvis Presley and Marilyn Monroe. All people I'd never met.

I'm convinced that the three losses changed me a great deal. I remember after my mum died I became temporarily convinced there was no God and the whole period certainly hardened me in many of my attitudes.

It was just so very hard to get my head round what was going on. I was left with an anxious feeling over what might happen next.

I think that in some ways having lost both my parents and one of my best mates in such a short time made me cling more closely to Jackie and that was a good thing.

Jackie herself was very quiet about what had happened which led some to think it hadn't affected her too much. To be honest I think it was just her way of coping.

Our marriage continued to be a combination of the blissfully enjoyable and the stormy. I think the traumatic events led me to go out a lot more than I should have and that was something Jackie used to get upset about.

Rather than go out a couple of times a week, I wanted to be out every night drinking champagne and having meals out.

Instead it was the simple things that gave us the most pleasure during our life in Lois Avenue: Walking our three dogs at night before going back to the house for a tasty supper, or buying nutty brittle from a sweet shop in Derby, or enjoying a beautiful salad on a sunlit Sunday afternoon.

I also remember happy Saturday afternoons watching Westerns with some of my mates, with Jackie making the sandwiches and happily condoning the lads at play.

It was when we moved to Hillside, beautiful house though it was, that things started to go against us.

We thought we could take a step up in lifestyle from our modest terraced house and proceeded to look for the trappings to go with it.

Perhaps if we'd settled for simplicity, our story would have been very different.

Chapter 4

A Shock 'Life' Sentence

NATURALLY, I've been in a few more than average scrapes with the police in my time. But, with some discretion and a fair bit of luck, I've always stayed on the right side of the law, which is now so important in times when doormen are nationally badged and can be removed for any criminal offence.

It was then a complete shock to me when at the age of 42 I faced up to prison. Yet it had nothing at all to do with the police. It still seems unbelievable to me that, having committed a "crime" that amounted to little more than failing in business, I could be locked up with some of the most hardened criminals – but that's exactly what happened.

I had been running Abacus Antiques with my wife, Jackie, since I was aged 26. We operated mostly from our home in Hillside, although we did have the luxury of a registered office in Sherwood, a very useful base for storage. Business was generally very good as I, in particular, learnt more and more about antiques and how to turn my knowledge into hard cash. Those were genuinely exciting times as I used to respond to calls from all over the Midlands and beyond and would calculate on the way home how much money we would be likely to make. My mistake was not to spread my bets a little wider in order to counteract times when the market was not so favourable. I've learnt since not to put all my financial eggs in the same basket and that explains why I have since gone back both into plumbing and the doors.

We took legal advice and, in line with many businesses at that time and since, decided to become a limited company. Jackie was made a director and I became the secretary, although, in reality, I was always the driving force behind the business. For a while, as the bottom eventually began to fall out of the market, we tried to mask our plight by selling some of our prized antiques. But, once you start to go financially downhill, it really can be a slippery slope from which you find yourself incapable of clambering up and out.

I still remember when my eyes first caught sight of the warning letters from the VAT people. Part of the problem was that a person I'd been doing a lot of my trade with had failed to produce the promised exemption certificates. I'd estimate that my debt to the VAT people and the Inland Revenue was never more than about £2,000.

To be honest I could probably have gone close to settling the debt fairly quickly, but once it has gone to court you're in trouble. They close down the company and freeze your bank accounts, so there isn't a lot you can realistically do. The bailiffs came round before the case went to court. They wanted to inspect our house to see if there were any assets they could readily seize. Things predictably got a bit lairy. I knew they had no legal right to come into my property, at that stage, so there was no way I was ever going to let them in. I told them that, if they called at my door, I would deck them.

Instead, I suggested, they could call at our office in Sherwood the following morning at 10am and I'd meet them there. They duly arrived to look round the building and then left – no doubt to report back to their masters from the Board of Trade that there was nothing they could take. Ironically, in the end they were to get all they wanted and more. When our house was eventually sold, it handsomely cleared our debts without us receiving a single penny of the change. The problem was that when an organisation like the Board of Trade get on your case, they then start digging for more dirt and the waters soon become very murky.

I recall the first time they phoned to say they were going to investigate our case. It was an eerie feeling, almost as though all the lights had suddenly been switched off in our house. I had to go into town to see them for the first time and Jackie went with me. It proved to be just the beginning of a long and very dark road. The poor woman was already very nervy and shaken up by it all as we were interviewed in a Board of Trade office by an awful man with a smirky, smug demeanour and black, dirty fingernails. Had it been a different time and a different place, I'd have happily frightened the life out of him. The meeting lasted about an hour and he took a fair amount of delight in telling me that I could well end up serving time. Considering that Jackie was present, he could have put things more carefully and tactfully, but that clearly wasn't his style.

The letters soon started to become more frequent and we were required to attend court. I say we because, at that stage, although her position as director was a front, Jackie was probably as liable as I was. Altogether I appeared four times before Jackie even got wind of the extent of what was going on. I made excuses that she wasn't well enough to attend when the truth was I hadn't even told her about it. Unfortunately, all I was doing was buying time. The court then warned me that they would issue a bench warrant for her to appear, so there was nothing left for me to do but to tell her. It was a terrible shock for her as I spilled the beans while Jackie was putting on her make-up one morning ready to go to work.

"Sorry, love, but we're going to have to go to court today," I said. "Why?" she replied, almost as a reflex action. I duly explained the grim details. The reason I left it until the very last moment was that I didn't want to even give her even one night in which to worry about what was going to happen. I honestly was scared stiff that, if she was put under too much stress, she might do a runner and that was the very last thing I wanted. The court proceedings were very short and all Jackie had to do was to answer some factual questions about whom she was. Nevertheless I knew it was a big trauma for her to go to court. As we were heading out, she was naturally very concerned and already wondering what the consequences would be. When she asked me whether we would end up in jail, I merely laughed it off and said it would never come to that. But my gut feeling was actually telling a very different story. I knew, almost from the beginning, that I'd be going down. The best I could do was to take her shopping to try to get her mind off things for a short while. They tell me that retail therapy can work wonders for the fairer sex at least!

Just to heap more pressure upon pressure, I managed to get myself into trouble with the police in another area of my life. I'd already had a close shave with the long arm of the law when I was stopped in my car by an officer in Clifton, near Nottingham.

Not being in the best of moods, I exploded in rage at him and had to take some knowledgeable advice from a mate and go down to the station to apologise for my behaviour. Nevertheless I still believe that incident had something to do with my conviction for drink driving a few weeks later. Jackie and I were driving home from the city where I'd had a few glasses of wine. I wasn't drunk by any means, but I was just over the limit and that was enough. That night I clung to Jackie as closely and dearly as I'd ever done and she did everything she could to assure me that she still loved me whatever lay ahead for both of us. I served a one-year driving ban during that terrible time and you can only imagine how much that did for my disposition. It meant also that, at a time when we were fighting for our financial lives, I was dependent upon my wife for getting to places.

Such a situation is all very well, in principle, as Jackie was only too willing to help me out. But, in practice, there were always going to be problems. Understandably, Jackie wasn't around 24 hours a day just to chauffeur me around. Then there was the fear of what would happen if we had an argument. Needless to say, during this time I did miss out on a reasonable amount of business purely because the antiques trade is very competitive and demands an immediate response. As they say, hesitate and the sale is lost.

At least not having to worry about my car anymore made it more convenient to hit the bottle. This I started to do most nights in a bid to dim the pain. The problem, as many people know to their cost, is that alcohol never quite accomplishes what we think is on the label. Sure it makes you a little happier while you are drinking it and therefore takes your mind off your worries, but there's the awful kick-back the following morning. I'm not just talking about the inevitable headaches, but the low you get from taking what is actually a depressant. Needless to say that at that time of my life I was not in a mood to see sense. The people from the Board of Trade were guaranteed to wind me up and that's just what happened. I despised them from the start and admittedly wasn't very co-operative.

There were two men actively involved on my case. I've already mentioned one – he'll be a lot better off if he never bumps into me again – and there was also a former police officer. There was a marked difference between the way they handled things, The ex-policeman seemed to put things into a more accurate perspective pretty quickly.

"You're not a bad bloke. You've just cut a few corners here and there," he concluded. I couldn't have put it much better myself. The only problem was that in the eyes of the Board of Trade, whose opinion mattered more, I must have been a real criminal.

On one notable occasion, when I saw this suited figure coming up the garden path I didn't bother to go to the door but sent my three Labradors out to greet him instead. He got a bit more than he had bargained for that day. Perhaps if I'd been more helpful I might have been spared some of the pain. But I treated them in much the same way as they treated me; like a piece of s---. I don't think that even to this day I know the full extent of the damage that those three stressful years caused me. For one thing, I never had much idea how long the whole process was going to take. It was like having a dagger hanging over you and being unable to know when it was going to fall. I just tried to put my blinkers on and keep going both for my sake and largely for Jackie and the family. If I had seemed full of panic and fear, they would have picked that up and suffered more than they did. It is a way of coping I've had to repeat throughout my working life – but not one that I would wholeheartedly recommend. Believe me, it takes a huge toll on your nervous system.

Finally, after what seemed like an eternity, the case went to Crown Court just before Christmas 1984. I faced around six or seven charges, largely relating to company law and the fact that I'd played too big a role in a limited company. I was advised that, if I pleaded guilty, I would not be sentenced until the following March and, more importantly, Jackie would be kept out of it. It was a deal worked out between us, yet when the prosecutor addressed the judge the way he put it was that they would not be pressing ahead with charges against Jackie because she was not well. Sounds familiar?

Looking back on it, I feel as though I was let down at this important stage of the case and still feel very angry and bitter about it. That

Christmas was a very strange time for both of us. There was a lot of emotion flying around and I remember that Jackie bought me a lot of presents. But there was no way good old Santa could get what was hanging over us out of our minds. We both knew, I think, that there was to be no turning back. It even affected our normally active sex life, so the stress of the case was beginning to drive us apart even then. Hardly surprising, really, when Jackie must have been wondering about whether she was going to have a roof over her head. It is amazing how fast the clock tends to tick when time is limited.

No sooner had the Christmas decorations been tidied away and New Year celebrations had drifted into the memory before, it seemed, March was upon us. The night before the case was one I will always remember. I drove to a pub in Nuthall Road with every intention in the world of doing a runner. In my mind I would be going to Scotland, but don't ask me why. I just wanted out of the whole mess. If I got away from it all – far enough, perhaps, for the authorities not to find me – I could get the chance to put the previous three years of constant worry behind me and start again.

A stumbling block in my mind, naturally enough, was Jackie, the children and my three dogs. I loved them all and the last thing I would have wanted was to be separated from them. But in my stressed-out, incoherent mind I almost came up with a satisfactory answer. Jackie would be better off without me and the almost constant trouble I seemed to attract, I contended. Yes, if I went away, it would be good for me and do no harm to those around me. I only had about £400 to £500 to my name but I gathered some antiques into my car, which I thought would help to tide me over whilst I got on my feet again. Not surprisingly, I sunk quite a few pints that evening as I tossed and turned in my mind whether I'd be heading north or back home. I remember that I still hadn't really made up my mind when I got back into my vehicle. I drove towards the ring road, still in the direction of the A1 and my planned escape route, then turned almost automatically left towards home. Perhaps instinct took over at that all-important moment.

I barely slept a wink. I remember being aware of virtually every hour on the clock, each being a step nearer to an occasion I was really dreading. I had a very clear sense of my destiny when I got up that morning. I stood in my garage and just knew I was going down. I walked along the path to our white Range Rover and handed Jackie the keys, plus all the money I'd put in my pocket from the previous strange evening.

"Why are you giving all this to me?" she asked. "Because I won't be coming back," I said, taking a last wistful look at the house I treasured so much. When we got to the multi-storey car park in Canal Street, I could hardly walk – my legs just felt like jelly. Jackie had been joined by my sister, Pat, in the gallery as the case opened. My barrister was full of promises. "There's no way you'll be going to prison today," he said. And, for a short while at least, I believed him. But when he returned to court later, having consulted with the prosecution, there was notably less eye contact and less sense of reassurance about his body language. I didn't enjoy the fact that it came out in court that I was a martial arts man. Made a good line for the Nottingham Evening Post, but what had that got to do with the way I ran our accounts? The picture they painted was of a man who had been unco-operative and volatile during the investigation.

When the Recorder came to his summing up I feared the worst. He spoke for several minutes, but it seemed like an eternity. He went on and on about how one charge alone could carry a sentence of two years and the other charges could mean this or that. Hastily totalling up in my mind, I thought I was going to go down for eight years! You don't want to have to suffer the preliminaries when all you are interested in is the punchline – and that was how long I'd actually have to serve. When he announced it would be 12 months I felt sick inside. At that moment I was led away, a convicted man and a prisoner, not to the security of my home but to a totally alien environment with my whole future hanging precariously in the balance. I could already see the tears welling up in Jackie's eyes and there was nothing I could do to stop them. I was just taken from the dock unable even to say a fleeting goodbye to the woman I loved. It was a feeling of helplessness I was to become all too accustomed to over the next long months. This promised to be the beginning of a traumatic enough separation after almost 20 years of marriage. But I didn't realise then that it was actually the beginning of the end for us. I would miss her so much during the dark days that lay ahead, not least the physical intimacy we so enjoyed. My prison term was obviously a very difficult time for Jackie and the children – my son Darryl was 19 years old when I went to jail and my daughter Lisa is just one year younger.

To some extent my life, volatile as it was, was set out for me. I had my accommodation, such as it was, and my three meals a day, if you could call it food, but Jackie no longer had any certainties or security in her life. She was having to think not only about herself but the children and the three Labradors. What did the future hold for all of them? All this because the Board of Trade had got their man. They had dug their claws into me when the initial complaints had come in and seen the case through to its conclusion – successful for them, but terrible for me. I honestly think that I suffered more than if I had been a murderer, a rapist or even a paedophile. I lost everything important to my life through that case and all over a few thousand pounds and a series of technicalities.

People have spoken to me since and told me that I'd fallen foul of the Freemasons. That's a theory I have had for some time as I honestly felt that I'd been well and truly stitched up. Funny handshakes or not, my face certainly didn't fit, that's for sure.

Being in prison was almost like being in a parallel universe. Life goes on in the real world, but you get to know little about it and there is nothing at all you can realistically do. The irony of the fact that it cost me my wife, my house and my increasingly happy existence was not lost on me as I'd done too much to attempt to keep Jackie in the dark. Yet it was that type of attitude, never wanting to confront the real truth, that heaped trouble upon trouble. Looking back on it all now I think that the three-year Board of Trade investigation with all its twists and turns probably did me as much harm as prison itself. Certainly the whole drawn-out process aged me considerably physically. This was I think a result of the near-constant worry, not only of what was going to happen to me, but also Jackie and the family. The way I tried to handle it was by protecting my wife from everything. In retrospect I now realise that was probably the wrong thing to do. It helped to develop her dependency upon me, which probably made life that much harder for her to bear when I was no longer around. In particular, I recall the endless morning tiptoeing down the stairs to ensure that I got to the morning's post before her. There were several occasions when Jackie came close to knowing just by my nervy reactions that there was something seriously wrong.

There was nothing, however, I could do to shield myself from the feelings I got when I faced up to my first moments in captivity. I was taken from the court to one of the police vans to begin the journey from Nottingham to Lincoln Prison. We got to Newark and I told the officers I needed to go to the toilet. So there I was, still hand-cuffed, being led from the van while onlookers edged away from me, reacting with apprehension and awe as if they had a killer in their midst. It just devastated me. What followed was pretty awful too. I'm sure most of you can recall the semi-comical start to the popular Porridge programme on TV when Ronnie Barker, or Fletch, is introduced to his fate. Well, there was nothing remotely funny about being confronted with the awful, imposing sight of the huge gates of Lincoln Prison. The very moment that the gates clanged behind me, my mind started to play some very unwelcome games with me. Now that my freedom had been taken away, what would happen next? I could meet my death behind these gates and nobody would know or, perhaps, now they'd got me they'd find something else out about me and lengthen my sentence still further.

I got out of the security van and immediately the staff were at me like a rash. Their task is to convert you from the man or woman you were on the outside to the lowest form of prison life and they do it with ill-disguised relish. I was put in a pen in the reception area that was more fit for a race horse. I was told to strip and my few remaining belongings were taken off me. I felt totally humiliated. In return, I was handed my prison uniform – a blue and white striped shirt, grey trousers and black shoes – and my survival pack consisting of blankets, a pillow, shirts and pants and not a lot else.

Then there was a lecture on the many prison rules, which make the Ten Commandments seem jolly. The next experience was terrifying. I was scared stiff of being locked up, a throwback to the claustrophobia of my youth, and the feeling just multiplied into blind panic as I approached my cell. It didn't help a jot that, as the induction routine had lasted several hours and it was now around 10pm, I was very tired on top of the stress of the day.

I told the guard my fears and he roared back: "Get in there now, or I'll put you into a straitjacket instead!" There was not a hint of any humanity in his words. But that's not untypical of many of the staff there. It was again at this point that I began to realise how isolated I was. Suddenly you're in there on your own, minus your wife, children, friends or any smiling faces, and it truly is a case of sink or swim. When I woke up the next morning and incoherently tried to make out the unfamiliar noises in the background, my first thought was that it had all been a dream. Then I saw the nightmare of a face pressed up against my cell door, shouting: "Get up you f------ b------!"

Welcome to the nick, Don. This certainly ain't going to be a holiday camp. But the thing that really brought it home to me that I was there to stay was the first time I emerged from my small cell. For on the outside of the door was the label 'McCalman – 12 months'. My cell itself was the scruffiest hell-hole of a place you could imagine. Uncomfortably small, it contained three bunk-beds, all with the cheapest 'blanket' sheets which were rather like having a sack bag around you. Everything about the place seemed designed to convince you that you were the lowest of the low. A bucket acted as our out-of-hours toilet. That meant that, if any one of the three of us answered a call of nature during the night, we were left with a smelly reminder of it until morning. The toilet ritual during the day did little more for me. We were led in lines towards the urinals and watched as we did our business. It all added to the sense of utter humiliation.

Particularly at Lincoln, the food itself was pretty terrible. Typically we'd get one piece of bacon and a slice of toast in the morning, followed by the likes of cabbage and potatoes at lunchtime. All very sparse and unappetising, Then, to complete the daily feast, we'd be served a cup of tea from a bucket at night. Rumours that the bucket had been spat in, or still worse, did very little to aid the digestion.

The sounds of cups being lowered down from one cell to another soon became another regular irritant. It was all part of the regular swapping of items between the prisoners.

At first, my routine was to be locked up for 24 hours a day, save for the meals and two meagre 15-minute exercise breaks. I soon volunteered to work in the net shop in order to get free of my cell for four to six hours, then there was the 'sanctuary' of the weekend church service. I don't think any of us had the slightest interest in what was being said – it was just another way of getting out for a while. Oh, and at Moreton Hall where there was another attraction of this impromptu form of church, some lovely butterfly cakes made by the ladies! To be honest, prison didn't do too much for my belief in God. In fact, I was more interested in asking the Almighty, or whoever might be up there, how on earth I got to be in that hellish place. I could have thrown in a few more burning issues such as natural disasters and wars between religious groups, but I was more concerned about the fate of number one at the time. I do thank prison for at least one thing – it did cure my fear of claustrophobia. I'd always had a great fear of doors closing behind me and my being left in darkness and would still prefer to this day to avoid using lifts if there is a half-convenient alternative. But one thing you discover in the nick is that you are very short of choices.

The shock 'treatment' achieved far more for me overnight than months of counselling ever did.

I did the rounds during what turned out to be a nine-month stretch. I was behind bars in Lincoln, a beast of a place, for the first six weeks, Ramby, near Retford, for two-and-a-half months, an overnight stay in Brixton for my appeal, a memorable one-nighter back in Lincoln and then to Moreton Hall for the remaining five months. People say very different things about prison life – some tell you it's hell on earth, others say it's more like a holiday camp. The one piece of advice I'd offer is: don't listen to people who've never been there when they pontificate about such stuff. I've been there and worn the T-shirt and reckon it does live up to its billing as a good deterrent. The main hurdles you need to adjust to are the loss of personal freedom, which when your life is collapsing around your ears on the outside can be no easy thing, plus the type of people you meet in there. The prisoners themselves more often than not are disgusting, scum-of-the-earth creatures whom you'd never voluntarily want to rub shoulders with.

The only way to deal with them is exactly the same way you work as a doorman. You need to be on top of them at all times. Any sign of weakness and they'll pick on you endlessly. If I found my stuff going missing, I'd jump on whoever was doing it straightaway and let them know in no uncertain terms that they'd be dead if they messed with me. A fearsome reputation spreads as quickly as a soft one in the nick and you soon get the message through.

I stuck together with lads who were in Moreton Hall for similar offences, rather than mix with the real thugs. We'd chat about how we couldn't believe we were in prison at all and promised each other faithfully that once we were all back out again, we'd keep in touch. But, with the notable exception, of Jamie Knapp, who became a good friend, it was never really going to happen. One consolation there was my £2 a week I used for buying sweets. You certainly learn to forget about money worries when you are in the nick.

Lincoln, in particular, was a shithole. Sorry about using that word, but how else can you really describe it? It was a real throwback to Victorian times with attitudes to match. Not surprisingly, perhaps, it was also home to some very hardened criminals. The lad next to me in my cell was a murderer and I found it very hard to handle the inhumanity of the whole place. The prison staff never looked upon you as though but for the grace of God it could have been them. Not for one second. Instead they treated you like crap, taking great delight in rubbing our noses in it at every conceivable opportunity. Some people naively think that, if anything goes wrong, you can confide in the staff. But not in my experience. Watching a film called 'Scum' on TV recently jogged a few memories. There was a prisoner crying out for help, but the 'screw' adamantly ignored him as he got more and more desperate. To be honest with you, some of the staff – and I am limiting it to some – are very sadistic people and take great delight in the awful plights of others. They hide behind their position and power, because I'm convinced that if you met them in the street they'd be a nobody.

There is at least one person, whose name and identity I'm keeping to myself, whom I'd still love to bump into to this very day. He would certainly find out more about the real Don McCalman. Just one example that seems like a small thing, but meant a lot to us at the time. We had a chance to watch a Pink Panther film. Now I wouldn't exactly call myself a fan – I'm a great stickler for 'reality' films in the sense that I like stories to be true – but the film was about halfway through and I was beginning to get into the plot. Then one of the staff turned the film off and ordered us all back to our cells. There was no conceivable reason for his actions, other than that he was showing us yet again he had the power to treat us how he wanted. That type of thing can get very wearing after a few months.

I did begin to win over some of the staff as time progressed. They knew I didn't do drugs and wasn't about to murder someone and at Moreton Hall I was allowed to drive the tractors as I was less than likely to bunk off. There was even a bit of humanity on show when I really started to go through the mill. I put so much emotional importance on my appeal, which my solicitors had lodged within a week of my first going inside. I was walking around the field at Ramby picking up paper when an officer shouted out to me: "Mac, your appeal has come through!" That was sweet music to my ears and, better still, I had little or no time to wait. I was to be taken to Brixton overnight and the hearing was to be the very next day.

At last things seemed to be moving in my direction. I recall being taken to the assizes on The Strand where I fully expected I was going to be given the best possible news – I would be a free man again. Jackie was in the court room, too, looking beautiful, a big enough incentive alone to get out of there and back into civilisation. The hearing was brief, cold and disappointing. I was barely addressed at all as solicitors spoke to the three appeal judges who were sitting. There was precious or little explanation of what was taking place before one of the judges started to speak. What he said hit me like a bomb. My sentence was cut by just three months. I just couldn't believe it. I was given just a couple of minutes to speak to Jackie, who was understandably upset, before being led away to a taxi where I was escorted by a woman police officer and two screws.

"It might as well rain until September," Jackie wrote to me soon afterwards. She was poignantly repeating the words of a well-known song and reflecting that now it would be autumn, at least, before I'd be a free man again. At least she'd still be with me, or so I thought.

One memorable night back at Lincoln proved very thought-provoking. When I arrived back at the prison, and was taken into the reception area, I glanced at this very downcast-looking prisoner and said 'hello' to him. I'd seen him during my first spell at the jail, although I didn't know who he was and he didn't answer me. Next morning the officers were late moving me back out of the jail and, when I got out of my cell, I saw guards taking a dead man out in a body bag. It was the same person I'd seen the previous night. He had committed suicide. I found out afterwards that it was Graham Neal, the Radio Trent disc jockey. In a very well publicised case at the time he had made a very emotional plea on behalf of his loved one, then subsequently been found to have been the murderer himself.

Thinking hard about what might have happened, I feel some measure of sympathy for those people who commit crimes of passion and even understand why others take their own lives. It is all so easy for others, who have never encountered such circumstances, to say they could never kill. But I've discovered that every one of us has an emotional limit and, if we're stretched too far, we can snap. Just a few minutes out of your usual sound mind and you might wreck or even end your life. Believe me, there are all sorts of people behind bars and not all, by any means, are real criminals, as the general public would understand the term.

It's difficult to pinpoint exactly when I began to realise that things were going wrong with my wife. Like a lot of women would probably say in the same circumstances, the feeling really just crept up on me. The visits, at one time once a fortnight, became less frequent and I got the impression Jackie was finding excuses not to come. I recall the dagger to the heart of building myself up for a visit and then one of the guards shouting out: "Sorry, she's not coming. Her car has broken down." Sadly, I suspected this wasn't true. The letters, too, that are a virtual life-support system for lonely folk in prison, became more sporadic and less affectionate in nature. Even the paper they were written on wasn't so good. You simply wouldn't believe the importance prisoners put on such communication. Let's face it, they get so little contact with the outside world. When the letters are being handed out and your name is not called it is as though you have been completely forgotten. It's terrible. Even now I've still got all the letters Jackie wrote to me whilst I was in jail – the good, the bad and the ugly. Back then, I read every one of them over and over again, checking for every ounce of meaning. But now I wouldn't dare read some of the later ones.

In my anxiety, I wrote to her sister, Natalie, and when the next visit came round she came along with Jackie. I said to my wife: "Talk to me." She told me that she didn't know whether she loved me any more. The words went through me like a knife to the heart and I desperately wanted to get to her, to hold her, shake her and change her mind. But the screws pinned me down and I was left a broken, shattered man.

It's amazing how your mind works when you're on your own with your thoughts. Jackie would consume virtually every waking thought. I'd imagine her in every possible situation. One moment I'd see her in my mind in the arms of another man, then, in a more optimistic mood, I'd picture her putting on her make-up ready to come to see me. Time would go very slowly in a prison cell and, just like I am now 20 years later, there's probably too much time to reflect for your own good. I'd run through a thousand times over what I'd say to her when I saw her again. Yes, I'd have it out with her and get to the bottom of it all. But, on the other hand, I'd be kind and loving and promise her that nothing like this would ever happen again. In this mood you don't really want much contact with anybody and are very unlikely to open up to relative strangers, even if they, more likely than not, are going through similar things themselves. You feel, however illogical this may sound, as though you're the only person who is suffering.

Fortunately I had my one and only home visit coming up, but again it left me with more questions than answers. The first strange twist was that Jackie told me that she couldn't get the day off work, so she would not be able to pick me up. Hardly the eagerness of a woman longing to see her man. Instead I had lunch with my daughter before going back home. By now Jackie was there and I swept her upstairs where we had sex. You can only imagine how good that felt after several months without any physical intimacy. This is a side of life you simply have to shut off when you are in prison, where the only sex on offer is either man-to-man or the do-it-yourself variety. Let's put it this way: if any dark and handsome male had stared longingly into my eyes I'd have ripped his head clean off his shoulders. Sorry about all that political correctness nonsense, but as far as I'm concerned God created Adam and Eve, not Adam and Steve. And I'm not one for creating my own sexual fun either. To me, it's either real sex or nothing.

However, Jackie's reaction afterwards soon took away the usual after-glow. She reacted in the sort of clinical way you'd imagine a prostitute would shrug off just having sex with a client. She merely picked up her clothes and strolled into the bathroom to have a bath, hardly saying a word. It was as though what she was doing was to remove all the physical effects and memories of the lovemaking away. Then, when it was time to go back to jail, she seemed unrealistically keen to whisk me away.

There was still time for a few drinks down one of my locals on the way, time to chew over the events of a day that I'd looked forward to for so long. Maybe I was wrong after all and Jackie was merely finding it a little difficult to adjust to having her man back, albeit for such a short time. Perhaps it was me who was being hard on myself by building the day up too much, by having expectations that were simply too great. Yet those thoughts again bit the dust. Once more the softer, loving Jackie had been replaced by a more cold, business-like approach. It was almost as though she was my taxi driver and the height of her concern was to ensure I got back to the nick in good time so she could pick up her next fare. The atmosphere was quiet and tense in the car and, as we drove up to the prison gates, I was longing for her to say something for me to hold on to. Just a word that she couldn't wait to see me again or was missing me would have eased so many of my fears.

I said: "When I get out of this dump, I'm going to get myself on my feet again." I thought she'd be pleased I was sounding so positive. Instead she snapped: "There you go. You'll be starting in business again. You'll never change!" And, to make things worse, when she handed me over, she told the officer I'd been drinking. Needless to say I was very tight-lipped with everyone about my home visit and immediately started fantasising again. The governor, spotting my distress, came up to me the following day and said: "Did you have a good day out?" He was worried that I might make things even worse for myself by doing a runner and, to be fair, that certainly was in my thoughts. I'd even managed to stash away £50, collect a few clothes together and was all set to go. It wouldn't have been too difficult as Moreton Hall was an open prison and anyone could just have walked free. Instead I started to compose in my head a letter to my wife that would finally clear the air and get us firmly back on the straight and narrow. At least the letter became a reality. In it I asked my wife if everything would be all right between us once I got out. To my huge delight she answered 'yes' and even spoke about us getting a new place together, to effectively make a new start. You can imagine how I took this and I spent the next few hours and days mentally thinking about our new house and how we would be back together as the happy family I recognised before all this awful stress and tension took over our lives. But I was on an emotional rollercoaster now and the dominant part of the journey was down.

When she came to visit again, I could tell from the moment she walked through the door that all was not well. Gone was the usual spring in her step, together with the fastidiously-kept appearance and the ready smile on her face that I'd envisaged when she was replying to my letter. Instead she almost shuffled into the room, looking nervous and unhappy. This was certainly not the time to compliment her on her losing weight as I guessed pretty quickly that she'd probably not been eating because of worry and having too much on her mind.

This time she told me that she really didn't know what she wanted and everything about her spoke of some kind of inner torment that she obviously didn't want to share with me. She looked emotionally shattered as though she had come to the end of a particular road and scarcely had the energy to turn round and start again. Inside I could only come to one conclusion – the reason for her uncertainty and distress with me was that she must be seeing someone else. I just didn't know who he was, but was going to give it my best shot to find out. I must have gone through virtually every man I knew and certainly everyone I could remember Jackie speaking to as I went over and over the same circles in my mind. The temporary relief of coming to some conclusion as to why it couldn't possibly be 'him' would immediately be replaced by the realisation that, if it wasn't, it must still be someone else. You can imagine how wound up I was getting as it came toward the time of my release. What an awful irony it was that the moment I'd looked forward to with such great intensity ever since I'd seen that first prison door close behind me was now so heavily compromised by the fear of what I might be about to discover.

Fortunately, my friend Alan Dennis, who came to pick me up, must have picked up some of the smoke signals from my cell. I could see the real concern on his face as, instead of greeting me with a big smile and a word of congratulations on my release, he said: "Just one thing, Don, just promise me now you won't go off your head." Funnily enough that was just what I'd had in mind. It seemed like ages as his car weaved its steady way through Nottingham, but eventually we were approaching our house in Hillside, Lenton. Strangely enough, and this wasn't at all how I'd imagined it, I was greeted instantly by my three large Labrador dogs. Oh, how I'd missed them, even if I'd thought of very little in the world other than Jackie for several weeks. And it was of some comfort at least that they, at least, seemed to have missed me, too.

Then came the moment I'd been waiting for. I swept into the house and laid eyes on Jackie for the first time. "You bastard!" I blurted out. Not the most romantic greeting, I readily agree, but it matched my feelings better than anything else I could think of. I saw my wife flinch a little, but there was never any danger of me laying a hand on her. That's just not my style. I've always hated violence to either women or children and have frequently meted out my kind of justice if I've seen it happening. Yes, I could and often did go off my head, but hit a woman? Never in a million years – there just isn't any excuse for it. Looking back now I can't say that I really blame my wife for what happened. I'd protected her, cosseted her and probably made her dependent. What had happened whilst I was in prison was that she'd reached out for that same security in another man – one who wasn't in trouble like I was. The next few days, as you can imagine, were a very mixed blessing.

Coming out of prison was one thing, but gradually realising that the cost was going to be losing my wife was quite another. Jackie did actually say "it's good to have you back" but, within a week, she was on her way to Spain for a holiday without me. I drove to East Midlands Airport to bring her back and asked all the usual questions, such as whether she'd had a good time. Her new man hadn't been with her. But, soon enough, I discovered a letter from him revealing that he'd been on a separate holiday at the same time. He said he wondered who would be the browner when they got back together. I was sick to the stomach, totally devastated. Jackie asked me whether I wanted to go out with her for the night. I instinctively said "yes", but could it really be the same? In fact it was simply awful. There was no closeness between us any more. When we went to a club, she told me not to stand with her. It was as though she didn't want to know me at all and was disowning me in front of others. We went home that night to our separate rooms.

Generally I used to go out for a few drinks and Jackie got home late. But there was the odd chink of light. One evening, when Jackie was home earlier, she took me a meal out on the patio and again said she was pleased to see me. I had no reason to doubt she meant it. On another occasion, when I'd been out with the lads, I'd imagined, for some reason, that Jackie would be there waiting for me, as in the good days. Instead she was out and came back still later, shuffling to her bedroom alone. Part of me longed to pluck up the courage to open the door and claim my wife back, but I just couldn't.

Within a week the tension had become unbearable. I just had to know more. I found out through some contacts where her boyfriend was living, picked up a public phone and said: "This is Don McCalman. Do you know who I am?" Those words would still send a shiver down a good many people to this day and, naturally enough, I didn't mind if they had the same effect here. We arranged to meet in a pub. I say 'arranged,' although I didn't give him too much of a choice. I said in so many words that, if he didn't meet me and sort things out, I'd bring my wife to him and drop her on his doorstep. You see, I'd made my mind up, I wanted her out and that was final. I couldn't live with a woman who'd been shagging behind my back whilst I'd been in prison. So was I being hypocritical, you say, considering that in the good days of the marriage I'd been no angel myself. I don't think so. It was the fact that there I was – imprisoned and with no possible way of fighting back. Jackie chose her path while I was in prison and, inadvertently, chose mine for me, too.

I went to The Planesman at Mapperley Plains looking for a handsome young man, with film star looks and huge personality who'd just swept my darling off her feet. The man who confronted me had nothing of the same image. He came up to me and said simply: "I'm Neil." It was brave of him. He could have had no idea that night whether my aim was to smack him to get revenge for what had happened. But I told him straight that he had two weeks to get Jackie out of the house. Since that first meeting I've come to realise that Neil is a genuinely nice guy. He's never objected to me phoning Jackie and he's been great with the grandchildren. In no way am I painting him as the villain of the piece. In fact, in some ways I'm pleased Jackie fell for such a man.

They both took me up on my ultimatum and the next few days were pretty terrible. My memory is of Jackie constantly packing, getting ready for her big day. When our house started to look bare and I began to echo around it like a ghost, it brought it home to me that this really was the end. I got a removal van for her. I was tormenting myself – and probably her – by playing soulful Phil Collins music whilst she was packing. Jackie was pleasant enough and even asked whether I'd like to go to her flat, which was in Sherwood. I said "no". Instead I went out to Wollaton Park for a long, reflective walk while she left. I don't mind telling you I cried a thousand tears. When I returned to the house I was hit for the first time by a feeling that has come to haunt me many, many times since. I was totally alone. Jackie had gone and things would never be the same again.

Chapter 5

Searching for Treasure

NOBODY, I suspect, would bat an eyelid if I said that my prime downfall in life was women – or even my explosive temper!

But, in all honesty, neither has caused me so much financial harm and anguish as following an obsession that has been part of my unpredictable life certainly since my early twenties – I'm talking, of course, about antiques.

It was my love of antiques that led me on the downward spiral that caused my imprisonment – however unfair I still consider that to have been – and then to lose both my wife and my home.

And even when I got out of the nick, I just followed the improbable dream even more. Magnificent obsession or just plain daft, I'm still not sure. It's difficult to put into a nutshell why logic can go out of the window when something as important as your own livelihood is at stake.

But I can only liken it to other compulsions. I consider myself to have been a massive gambler, although not in the way most people would recognise it.

The more conventional gambler may be beguiled with gaming machines or perhaps the horses. It doesn't matter how many times he hears the warning bells that success in the long term is unlikely – the compulsion is there and it drives him to go on and on.

Even the inevitable losses are merely a spur to try again. After all, if today has been a dreadful day, it is all the more important that you'll come up trumps tomorrow. And you know that, although the odds might be against you, literally anything is still possible. Looking back now, it's a real pity for my bank balance that I didn't spend some of my money on houses instead of antiques. I could have bought a row of houses with some of the money I've lashed out on advertising alone.

Yet there's always been something alluring and fascinating about antiques. Throughout my life I've been the kind of person who simply loves to walk around an old stately home, admiring not only the artistic value and beauty of the individual items but feeling that unique link with the past.

I've never quite made it to own my own stately home, so I suppose, sub-consciously, at least, I have done my best to create my own special place, as my houses have always been full of antiques. I feel like a combination of Long John Silver and Dick Turpin as I survey what to me is a potential treasure and lay my plans to bring it back home.

There's a joy, too, in the anticipation that's almost as exciting as the real thing. This is what whets the taste buds when you get an antiques call. I'll get just enough information to make me want to travel the sometimes long distances involved. Yet, genuinely, until you do see for yourself you have really no idea at all whether it is going to be worthwhile.

It all started for me when I was about 27 years old and went down to an antiques shop in Castle Boulevard, Nottingham, for the very first time. I took a look at this sewing machine, which was one of the first of its kind and was beautifully inlaid with pictures. It appealed to me straightaway for no better reason than it was old. So I parted with my £10 and went on to sell it for £20 – much more of a gain then when terraced houses were about £500 apiece and my profit was not far short of a week's wages.

Anyway I was soon well and truly hooked, even though I had no real idea what on earth I was doing. I went to a house and bought myself a lovely corner cupboard, again being taken so much by its sheer age that it seemed like an exciting item to possess. Nothing too much scientific about it than that.

I took another step on the road when I bought myself a grandfather clock. I'd always wanted to possess one as I loved the sense of history about them – their smell alone somehow puts you in touch with the past.

At that time, however, my heart was more in touch than my head. I was so naive that, as I was carrying it away, the hood came loose and gave me a fair old crack on the head. To be honest I hadn't even realised that could happen.

I hadn't a clue at that point about the different types of wood – whether an item I quite liked the look of was made from ebony, mahogany, beech or cherry was a mystery to me.

Everything I have learnt about antiques since has been self-taught or just the result of years of experience. Now I can size up a piece and say pretty well what it is made of and whether it was from then seventeenth or eighteenth century, or from the eras of George II or III, William or Mary and so on. And, more importantly, I can tell almost immediately what any item is worth to my client and what it is worth on the antiques market if and when I come to sell it.

At first, it was a bit of a hobby for Jackie and myself. We'd enjoy the thought that the proceeds were helping to fund a fairly good lifestyle in which I could take her out for a meal and we could choose what we really wanted. I just loved it and didn't think too much, at that time, of the inevitable peaks and troughs of the business.

One day I was making good money, the next I was on the slippery slope to destruction. Yet I wasn't in the mood to heed any warning signs and go back to either plumbing or the doors. We'd maybe travel to Sheffield the next day to look expectantly at the antiques on display in a particular house. I'd be weighing up the potential profits and she was determining what we might like to keep!

One of the items we both came to enjoy, albeit for contrasting reasons, was Victorian dolls. Jackie loved them whilst I was just interested in them for the money. I think at one point our house in Hillside was probably heaving under the weight of them, but, when the other lines of business were struggling a bit, we used to sell four a week and bring in about £400 in total. Very useful money whichever way you look at it. On good days with antiques I could be making £300 a day yet, even then, it was a total gamble. I'd get into my van, bound for exotic destinations as far afield as Wales, Doncaster and Leeds.

Trouble, however, was never far round the corner. There was this guy at Newark I used to sell stuff to. I rang him about a sideboard and he put in an offer of £1,300. The problem was that another man wanted it for £1,800. Out of courtesy, I tried to get back to my friend to see if he'd match the offer, but I couldn't get hold of him.

Anyway, after I'd sold the piece my friend blew his top and said he would never do any more business with me. That was ok, his loss, as I'd say. But one of his cronies went a whole lot further by bad mouthing around town that I'd threatened to shoot him. Now I admit to be fiery, but that's not my style. This was one of those Chinese whisper-style occasions when people add to what has been said and the original truth goes out of the window.

That time around a serious warning sufficed. I told him straight that if I ever heard anything like that said again about me he would be in serious trouble. Needless to say he never bought off me again.

There was always trouble brewing if people didn't settle their accounts. On one notable occasion three thugs came to visit me to try to make a point after a disagreement over some stuff their boss had sold to me. I took a bit of a beating, including getting clouted over the head with a lump of wood. I was forced to stay in overnight at Queen's Medical Centre where I nursed both my raging headache and wounded pride. I had the opportunity to speak to the police about what had happened but this was one dispute that needed sorting how it started.

A few days later, without Jackie knowing a thing, I drove over to Stamford, Lincolnshire, to speak to the source of the problem. As soon as he opened the door to me, I hit him like a brick. I left him in no doubt that, if he ever felt like sending any more thugs over, it would be the last thing he ever did. I told him there would be a free ride in an ambulance waiting for them next time because I would be ready for them.

Antiques are a very competitive business and can sometimes get you into trouble with the law. I have had the Old Bill on my case a number of times over the years, although usually I have been the innocent party.

One Saturday at about 8.15am there was a loud banging at the door of our terraced house. Two men and a woman were standing there and I asked if I could help them.

"Is your name Don?" asked one of the men." Yes," I answered. "We are police officers and we need to take you with us because Mansfield Police want to talk to you."

Soon I realised that this was no polite invitation – I was under arrest, but for what? I was taken into their police car and the woman officer steadfastly refused to speak to me during the journey. We arrived at Canning Circus police station where officers stripped me of my money and other valuables, still without any reasonable explanation.

I asked: "What the hell is going on?" Or it might have been a touch stronger than that! All they did was to repeat their original message that Mansfield Police wanted to talk to me. Eventually an officer and a detective arrived and I heard them murmur between themselves: "He doesn't meet our description. You better let him go."

I was relieved, of course, but insisted that, seeing as I'd had a chauffer-driven ride to the station, they really ought to do the decent thing and drive me home. Two officers on the way back seemed to be plugging me for information and this time the cat was let out of the bag. Apparently a man and a woman had been using the name of Abacus Antiques, the same as our business, to run a dodgy enterprise in which they had been calling door-to-door. Their method was that the woman kept the resident busy whilst the man went round the back and made off with whatever he could lay his hands on!

I offered my services there and then if the police wanted me to do the job for them and sort this dreadful couple out, but they politely refused. Instead what I did do was consult my solicitors to put out a public notice in the local paper distancing us completely from such activities. For the record, we never 'cold called' by going round the doors, but responded to people who contacted us.

Another incident that very nearly got out of hand was with a company I had plenty of dealings with in Nottingham. One of the partners told me they were going away for a fortnight, but their father would deal with me during their absence. I sold him some furniture, a clock and a few other smaller items, agreed a fair price and went on my way.

But when one of the sons came back from holiday, he said: "I want to have a word with you. We have paid you too much – but don't worry we'll just take off a little each time we buy from you in future." "No way!" I blasted back. "I sorted the deal in good faith with your dad and there's no reason to go back on it now." For good measure, I punched one of them onto a cabinet causing £100 worth of damage. I never had a problem with them again.

This was an incident I particularly remember because, when I walked out of the shop, I saw someone trying to grab my leather coat from my car. Had I been in a better mood, I might have opted for a quiet word – well, maybe! But, as you can imagine, my mood was entirely black, so I grabbed his hand and pulled it down onto the car. Then I punched him on the side of his head and left him slumped on the floor.

The territorial warfare among antique dealers can be quite intimidating – unless, of course, you're prepared to give them a taste of their own medicine in return.

My advertising net has always been spread far and wide and I had decided to publicise Abacus Antiques in a newspaper in Sheffield, South Yorkshire.

One evening I got a nasty phone call. "Are you the antique dealer? Well, get out of Sheffield or I'll kill you!"

I was in a combative mood and determined to get the better of him.

"Don't worry I know you and I knew your mother, too – she was on the game," I replied. I could sense full well the anger as the man seethed on the other end of the phone and realised he may not let this one drop.

I contacted the regional crime squad and told them of the threats I had received. They told me to be on my guard at home and even took the trouble to check up on me.

Instead the issue was solved my way. I was trailing down City Road, near the centre of Sheffield, with my mate Pat Clarke visiting a couple of antiques shops.

We went into this shop and I said to the bloke: "Have you ever heard about Abacus Antiques?" He answered: "Yes, I really put the fear of God into them. They won't be showing their faces round here."

Pat calmly shut the door, knowing what was coming next and not wanting an uninvited audience.

"I am from Abacus Antiques," I told him. "And if you ever phone me again, I'll burn down your shop!"

The mighty mouse was almost in tears as we left his shop.

With such things going on, it is hardly surprising that, although Jackie herself caught the antiques bug, she never got as passionately involved as me. She played a full part in our business, however, and, as I've said before, I protected her successfully against the Board of Trade during those awful years. The difference between Jackie and myself was, I think, that she learnt her lesson and I didn't.

I think that one of the reasons she moved on was the feeling that, after I came out of prison, I'd go feet first into something else and land us in trouble again.

She had seen what had happened to us. Whilst I was behind bars, she'd had to face the terrible truth that she was going to lose her home and, understandably enough, she didn't want to live like that for the rest of her life. I can't really blame her because basically she was right. I brought a lot of trouble into her life and antiques had been at the heart of some of it.

And my obsession with antiques was far from over after I got out of prison. Faced with the unappetising prospect from the probation service of moving into a hostel, it was my expertise with antiques that helped me get a deposit on my current property. I was struggling to get together a £2,000 deposit for a £31,000 house but the proceeds from a bureau, table, chest of drawers and a few bits and bobs came in very useful.

Within six months I had a Red XJS and within a year I was filling a home of my own with a mountain-full of impressive antiques. You don't necessarily admit such things at the time but by so conspicuously being a success with antiques again, I was making a point to my wife.

I've always wanted to be top dog whatever I've done and in the world of antiques this has been no different. So just as I've had my choice of the best cars and run the biggest hotel in Nottingham needing 15 doormen, I've always aimed my profile very high in business.

I've spread the word far and wide by advertising throughout the East Midlands counties of Nottinghamshire, Leicestershire and Derbyshire searching for the best – the best clocks, the best suites, the best desks and so on. The money I've speculated, or outright gambled, on antiques since that time has been so great I scarcely want to consider it.

To this day what I spend on advertising with Yellow Pages and British Telecom alone each year runs very comfortably into six figures each year. I could if I had wanted to have gone to auctions and made a fairly decent living, particularly with my experience and knowledge, but Don McCalman never does it that way. I know that it can't continue for much longer and that will undoubtedly be a great relief to my son Darryl, a much more practical businessman than me, who scowls every time I mention the size of my advertising bills. He told me that when he was younger he would see my advertisements and say proudly: "that's my dad doing that." But, as he got older and realised the amounts I was lashing at, it just made him cringe.

Just to give you another idea. I have advertised for many years in the Loughborough Echo, a weekly newspaper in the East Midlands, and spent a great deal of money with them. Sometimes I would get angry when I saw someone put in a bigger advert and increase mine purely for the sake of maintaining that number one slot in my own mind.

I honestly doubt all these years later whether I've even made my money back from all the advertisements. Rather than make me any wealthier, they have just sent my overheads to a sky-high level. If anything eventually finishes me in business, it has got to be advertising. In retrospect I might as well have put my money into a machine or even on the lottery because advertising is that much of a gamble.

To be honest it is all part of the financial enigma that is Don McCalman. If only I'd listened to my mother when she gave me the simple but blindingly obvious advice 'save the pennies, for pennies make pounds and pounds make hundreds'. I have been clever in the way I have made money in my life, yet I have always been a terrible manager. With my tendency to speculate and gamble, I have let so much money slip through my fingers – and for what?

Today I'm very much in two minds about antiques. Not so long ago I spoke to Jackie and she told me she'd never really liked them, but I'd never go as far as that. They've given me a lot of pleasure and they have suited my reflections on life perfectly. But, no, it has never been as exciting as people perceive it to be.

Often Denis will sit down on my couch whilst waiting for me as we go to work together in the morning and say something like: "How can you be so miserable when there's all this lot around? Others would die for a fraction of all this!"

But, then, what does it all really mean? I know, for certain, that I can't take any of it with me. That's a fact of life that even a tough guy like myself has to give second best to. I've thought of the subject a lot, not least when I've been to the houses of widows who want to clear both their properties and some of their memories.

Antiques tell you an awful lot about human nature. There was a lovely woman, a keen animal lover, who saw my advertisement in the newspaper and phoned me up so I could take a look at some items.

I bought some tables, silver and porcelain from her and a few months later she was back in touch again for similar reasons. She told me quite clearly that if and when something happened to her, she wanted me to have first look at her antiques to sell them for her favourite animal welfare charity.

Yet when she did pass away, all hell let loose. Her solicitor rang me to say I needed to go over, but when I did so there were no fewer than five other cars parked at the house. The woman had never even mentioned to me that she had any living relatives and, on all the occasions I visited, there had been absolutely no sign of any company.

Yet when she was dead, they literally descended like vultures picking over every last item and making me feel distinctly uncomfortable, as you might imagine. Needless to say, I have seen this particular gruesome scenario repeated many, many times and it gets no more palatable. It's almost as though people are just waiting for their relative to die and can't wait to go in and clear out the property.

I wondered then and again many times since if it would make so much more sense to sell off the valuables and live the good life for a change. My mate Dave Sankey is looking for a place in the country for me – a nice property with space to put my Bentley.

I could pay out a couple of years rent in advance and live in peace, financially secure. I have received offers for my antiques so that wouldn't be much of a problem. However I would be missing out on a mystical dimension in my life.

When you have visited some of the properties that I have – some of them absolutely mind-blowingly fabulous, others more homely and humble – you begin to appreciate the attachments people have had to their prized items.

If you consider the word 'antique', it literally means 'the past' and in my experience they often tell a fascinating story of times gone by. In my current collection I've got a clock that is an amazing 200 years old.

Maybe, I'm a bit fanciful but just listening to its distinguished chime takes me into a different world, particularly at night. I can just imagine in my mind's eye my lounge being taken over by the previous owners of all these many items, coming to take another look at their prized possessions and pointing out to the others whom they really belong to.

You might think I'm mad or soft, but these thoughts come from an appreciation of just how much emotion has been invested in them. And I believe that emotion and energy never fully goes away.

In the same way I'd absolutely love to spend the night in a haunted house, or even a castle. Again it is as though the events that have taken place in these surroundings and the people who have been involved in them are still alive. And what could tell a more interesting story than those antiques that have bridged past and present?

That's not to say that I don't have the odd chuckle or two when someone reads a little too much significance into what is going on.

Several times I've been in a house with a widow talking about the family's beloved grandfather clock.

"You know the strangest thing," she'll say as I prepare for mock surprise. "Ever since my dear husband died this clock hasn't chimed at all. It's as though the clock has died too."

Unfortunately the explanation is often much more down-to-earth. I'll have a look at the clock and discover that the reason the clock is still is that it hasn't been wound up since he died. I'm not being hard-hearted here, for some of these old clocks took a great deal of winding as they were very heavy and unwieldy.

Times, however, really do change and, whereas I could hardly disagree in the past when Jackie pointed out that possessions were my life, that is no longer the case today. This time I know full well that the market is in decline. The golden period for antiques in my experience was probably in the 1970s and 80s and it has been a gradual downhill curve since.

Both the number and the quality of the antique calls we are now getting is going down quickly. You can sense from some people's desperation to get rid of stuff that is little more than nostalgic rubbish that the boom period is over.

Just to give you an example from my own collection. I have a favourite Edwardian cabinet that just five years ago would have realised £500, but I wouldn't expect to get more than £150 for it today.

There may be more of a widespread, superficial interest in antiques, caused mainly by the proliferation of TV programmes about the subject. I'm referring notably to the very popular Antiques Roadshow, but that is now just one of several. In many ways I blame such programmes for putting a lot of people out of business and therefore out of work. I cringe when I get a phone call and the would-be client mentions that they have an item very similar to one they'd seen on TV, which was valued at a particularly high price. I'll tell them: "Well, sell it to the TV company then." This is because in the real world outside TV I know the original price was well off the mark in today's market.

The same applies to the Internet. People will phone up saying they saw an item on E-bay for £500, but that doesn't mean that is a realistic valuation. The honest truth, as I see it and remember I have been in the business a great deal longer than most of the media experts, is that the items just aren't there any more – good ones anyway.

Then, if you find a good rare piece of furniture, there's further frustration because it is very difficult to get a buyer for it. I believe the market is in terminal decline just as the country itself may be on the verge of recession. Whether it will recover in the future I'm not qualified to say, but I don't think it will do so in my lifetime.

At times I could well imagine an auction of all my stuff, whether I am still in the world or not, but I can't honestly say whether I'll sell.

I know for certain that I'm going to cut back my advertising on antiques hugely and just maintain a few local advertisements. People these days are almost desperate to get rid of prized items to meet their own bills, so there will always be some kind of market there.

I would swap anything and everything from my antique world for my children and grandchildren. I've learnt, albeit rather late, that it is living things that really matter in life – people rather than possessions.

The beaming smile on a young face, the childish question that brings laughter and an involuntary tear to the eye, these are the things that can make life worth living. Possessions can only give you so much pleasure. A clock can't give you a smile at the end of a difficult day and say "I love you."

My daughter phoned me recently and invited me to go and see my young granddaughter playing tag rugby. I can honestly say that I enjoyed that far more than viewing a thousand antiques. In the same way I keep all the drawings that my grandchildren have done – they are what life is really all about rather than famous paintings.

Yes, Jackie was right all along. She tried everything to tell me that I was on the wrong path by filling my life with things rather than people. But, like in everything, I've seen the light all too late. You can't turn the clock back, even the most beautiful grandfather variety, and now I'm living with a multitude of regrets.

Yet perhaps as I approach my final curtain I have discovered that there is real treasure out there after all.

Chapter 6

Heartbreak Hotel

THE JOURNEY on the lift going up to The Penthouse Bar on the eighth floor of The Royal Hotel in Nottingham seemed to take for ever.

Friday night had kicked off much as normal. I was heading about 13 doormen, including four in Grouchos and two in The Penthouse, with others covering all the various bars and restaurants.

But, however many times you do this job, there's nothing like the anticipation of responding to an instant SOS, having no idea what you are going to find.

I can't imagine quite what the guests made of it as I stood, an imposing figure in my black suit and dickey bow, flanked by two other massive doormen.

I made no eye contact with them at all as I stood bolt upright, totally focused on whatever was to come and rehearsing in my mind the way I was going to deal with it. As far as the guests were concerned, my priority, as always, was to ensure they had an enjoyable and happy evening, but free from rowdy anti-social behaviour. Giving an impression of being in quiet control of the situation – whatever that was – was my way of ensuring that I didn't spread any unnecessary alarm.

I watched the floor numbers with spellbound intensity. In just a few more seconds, the doors leading me to the magnificent Penthouse Bar would duly open and I'd need to size up the problem in an instant.

Countless were the nights when I'd sat with fellow doormen and guests at the end of a hectic evening, taken in some of the most fantastic views of the city of Nottingham and started to wind myself down for the shortish car journey home.

The Penthouse, with a capacity of 300 people, was one of the city's top social attractions in those days and my job was to ensure that guests who paid good money to stay at The Royal weren't left with unhappy memories of a night spoiled by drink-fuelled excesses.

Immediately the doors opened my eyes narrowed onto an idiot holding court in the middle of the bar area. I could recognise almost without blinking the alcohol-induced bravado as he held a half full beer glass in his right hand and eye-balled a group of youths with almost manic intent.

I could read the tell-tale signs like an experienced motorist reads a map. Just at this moment only one person was the undoubted hub of attention, but within seconds the argument would have spread like a fire taking its devastating and raging grip.

I must have looked like Batman as I entered the room, my colleagues giving me silent, but very imposing support.

Just a few purposeful strides and I was alongside the chief troublemaker. With a decisive movement I wrenched the glass out of his hand while he was in mid flow and said: "You're leaving now!" He turned round with a mixture of indignation and horror in his alcohol-bloated face and spluttered: "Give me my pint back mate. What's it got to do with you anyway?" He looked at his friends around the table for any indication of support, but was met only with sheepish, knowing grins. They weren't, after all, quite as drunk as he was.

"I'm the head doorman here and you are leaving," I said, simultaneously grabbing him and ushering him away from the crowd. I had little trouble overpowering him for, although he was a strapping lad probably in his mid to late 20s, I knew exactly what I needed to do and had my colleagues alongside me if anything got out of hand.

Soon enough, he was in the lift, offering by now no more than a few token oaths as resistance. None of us uttered a word as I held the man firmly in check and waited, more patiently this time, for the lift to click down to the ground floor.

The doors opened, we marched him a few more yards to the exit and, with a slight flourish, pushed him out of the door with a less than convivial: "Goodnight!" We watched for a few seconds as he gathered what remained of his wits and staggered off into the street.

That's just the sort of routine incident I've dealt with many a Friday and a Saturday evening at The Royal Hotel in Nottingham over the last 20 years.

And it illustrates in so many ways how I think the job of doorman needs to be done.

First and foremost in my mind are my bosses – the management of the hotel – and the guests who have paid to be there. I have always aimed at being a disciplined extension of the management's authority, knowing full well that if anything serious kicks off I'm the first person they would come to.

My work, let it be said, starts hours before such an incident starts. Like a true professional, I'd be sizing the evening up in my mind, possibly for days ahead.

As head doorman, a position I've held throughout my time at The Royal, my task is to ensure we have just the right level of security on the doors.

It might be a routine Friday and Saturday with the bars and restaurants open to guests and friends or there could be a special function on board such as a wedding party, a stag do or a dinner dance.

As I look at the details, perhaps over the fax machine, I fix my mind on what I feel is needed.

To cover The Royal when I first started out there I liked to have my 13 doormen.

Obviously some of the doormen's names come almost by second nature. They are the lads – and sometimes the lasses – who usually work week in week out with me and I can largely trust with my very life.

They'll work with me on one weekend shift, I'll pay them their dues, which to this day come to around £40 a time, and I know full well they'll be there for me next week.

But, inevitably, nothing runs quite as smoothly as that. There are holidays, illnesses, other reasons why people are unavailable or I may be unhappy with the idea that someone should be working the door this week.

Being a doorman is one thing, being a manager of your own team is quite another. Always I need to be one step ahead of everyone else, yet fully in control of what I'm doing too.

The ring-round for casual staff, at best, brings mixed results. I need three more reliable doormen to fill the gaps this weekend and all I've got so far is a series of unanswered calls, a couple of 'maybes' from potentially disappointed women folk and a cigar burn on a page of my over-used address book.

It's amazing how weeks always shape up like this. Even when you think it is going to be straightforward, I'm inevitably left hanging on almost until the last moment.

Finally I get my men. Two out of three ain't bad, goes the song, but in this case three out of 20 is about par for the course. I've made about 20 calls, including folk I've tried twice, and in the end I've got three 'definites' to man the doors.

It is much more difficult to fit the right man, or woman, to a door these days. In the past, I'd get out my address book and pick the person I thought was best suited to a particular venue, then just hope that they were available.

But it doesn't work that way any more. The fact that all doormen have to be badged is an unmistakable necessity and cuts down my options straightaway.

If you are caught doing a door without a badge, it is a criminal offence for both doorman and those in charge.

My job basically is to check with each person whether he or she is badged. That's where my responsibility begins and ends

But still there are worries and unpredictable things to sort out before the shift itself really gets under way. I recall that Pete was in a terrible state. He and his girlfriend had split up earlier in the week and he looked as though he was a man with a revenge mission.

When he turned up on the door, instead of being neatly turned out as usual, he had hints of a less careful appearance. His suit looked like it had seen better days – or rather hadn't seen the dry cleaners for a month or two – his hair was less than perfectly combed and there was a slightly wild look to his eyes.

I make a point of being Don, the boss, a man more likely to look straight through you with a piercing look than lend you an arm around the shoulder. But there are times when you need to know what's going on.

After a couple of half-hearted negatives in which he made one last attempt to hide his raging feelings, Pete told me what was happening. He'd been seeing this girl for six months or so and she hadn't minded a jot that he was a doorman. In fact it gave her extra kudos with her mates to think she'd caught the eye of one of those street-wise hunky bouncers that ruled the roost at such an upmarket and reputable location as The Royal.

But slowly and surely the emotional tide had turned. Knowing that Pete finished his shift at 2am meant she was happy enough when he collapsed home on the bed at 3am – but what possible reason did he have for coming in at 5am?

She'd asked me – if that's the right word – a similar kind of question at about 4am the previous Saturday morning.

"Where's Pete, I thought he'd be home by now. Doesn't he finish at 2am any more?"

Thoughts flashed through my head. I wished sometimes that I finished at 2am, she took it for granted that I'd still be here, but then she had no concern whether I had someone to come home to or not.

But the thought that dominated my mind was far different. She was about 5'6", a curvy, busty blonde with long willowy legs and a mini skirt that you couldn't take your eyes off if you'd been a priest. In short, she'd been following good-natured Pete for weeks and now she seemed to have caught up with him – at least I think that was what all the grunts, groans and moans were about as I tried to shield the phone from his girlfriend's ears.

At such times you wonder what it would be like to tell the truth. They say, don't they, that you should always be straight with people and use the sword of truth. But, on occasions like this, it would surely be more like a dagger through the heart. Pete didn't really deserve my sympathy, after all he hadn't exactly needed a chat on the birds and the bees. It takes two to tango and he hadn't looked as though he'd needed too much arm twisting.

All these thoughts and more would be whirling through my mind and were reason enough to tell the poor woman the harsh truth that Pete was shagging someone else. She'd put the phone down, be off my back and would probably be making eyes at another bloke soon enough. That's usually the way of the world.

But, no, she really wasn't my priority. It wasn't her who had given up her Friday and Saturday evenings for almost all of the last four years and put her body on the line. Pete was a good, solid doorman, well able to diffuse difficult situations and with an above-average amount of tolerance for the intolerable. What if, having had to put up with meatheads who wanted to smash his head with a bottle or loud-mouthed women who'd vomited over his cleanly pressed suit, he'd met someone with an ounce of humanity and, let's face it, tasty 36DD assets.

My task was to think of Pete. "No, love, we've had a few incidents kicking off tonight and he's helping me to clear up. He should be home in about 45 minutes," I answered, as calmly and unemotionally as if none of the above thoughts had ever entered my head.

At the end of the day, I have to protect my men and what they get up to after they have finished their shift is basically none of my business.

Equally, it is not going to help me very much, nor them, if I send them home to a make-or-break row with their missus.

You might disagree with me, but there are times when you simply can't tell all. And this is one of them.

No doubt some of my stories have not been totally believed by their girls, but that's not something I need to concern myself with too much.

I'd like to think that my approach has helped to heal more wounds than it has caused and kept more relationships and marriages together.

Anyway, as I explain at other stages of this book, I've been no angel myself and am no stranger to the fascination ladies have with doormen.

The phone replaced, I marched off to Pete. Thankfully he and his new beau had finished and looked a little relieved, if anything, at my belated intervention. "You silly sod, Pete," I said, as soon as the woman had got out of his hair.

"What do you think you were doing? I've had your misses on the phone in floods of tears. Guess what I told her? "

"No idea, boss," he spluttered. "I said you were working late, you daft bugger. But you might not be so lucky next time!"

The cheeky smile returned briefly to his care-torn face and off he went into the night. Hopefully to return chastened, but without having his fingers unduly burnt.

But clearly the old Don charm wasn't quite sufficient in this case. The unhappy couple were going their separate ways and I had a potential emotional time bomb on my hands,

Could I afford the risk of him exploding on some relatively innocent guest who made a remark that could be taken two ways? Or could I trust tonight's intake of eligible blondes with a man who looked as though he wanted to exact personal retribution on the fairer sex?

One thing was for sure, I knew for certain his mind wouldn't be on the job. Better one man down than the whole team go in the dock for Pete flying off the handle. I sent him home, but saying I expected the old Pete back next Friday.

There are two obvious views I could take in such a situation.

Firstly I could play the hard man and insist: "Turn up for work tonight, lad, on the dot, or you're out of a job."

I'd say just this if I felt that they'd be better off being on the job where they could turn their thoughts away from their domestic troubles. In effect, working would be a form of therapy for them.

It could certainly be a better option than hitting the bottle and attempting to drown out their sorrows.

On the other hand, they might seem so screwed up that I could easily imagine them losing their usual cool when dealing with awkward customers and take their pent-up frustration out on them.

That would be bad for them, bad for the customers and, worse still, bad for me.

Its precisely those kind of decisions that you can agonise about and, in the end, you just have to go with your gut feelings, based on what you know about the different characters involved.

Perhaps I, too, was carrying around more than a tinge of envy. Women of all shapes and sizes, but usually the right ones, had been queuing just a little too long to have a word with me, wanting to know who the Kenny Rogers-type character was. Wasn't I the plumber they'd seen in the street once? Was I as dark and moody when I was off-duty? You know the type of thing....

But, reluctantly, I'd pushed them away. Or rather I'd used my fellow doormen as a human shield. "He doesn't want to talk to you, love," one would say as I gestured that I wanted to be as far away as possible.

There was nothing wrong with them, of course there wasn't. But there was plenty enough going on inside me and none of it was for sharing.

The break-up with Jackie totally destroyed me. I knew that then when I started working at The Royal and I know it now, even more acutely perhaps, some 20 years or so later.

But, after leaving prison and finding my life in ruins with my wife, my home and my financial security all gone, a friend called Trevor said to me: "Don, why don't you go back on the doors? Come and work for me because you are good at what you do.

And I could think of no reason to argue.

I never expected to be go back on the doors. Not at all. I'd happily given it all up during my marriage to Jackie, but now I'd lost all the security in my life and besides I needed both the cash and the boost of being needed and wanted,

I think that sub-consciously, at least, I was already in the business of needing to prove something to Jackie. She had been scornful of me going back into business again after all my troubles, whilst I was desperate to put the past behind me by becoming a success.

Working on the doors was my way of filling that gigantic emotional void and, yes, proving myself all over again. To a man with my expectations, having to virtually start my life afresh at the age of 43 was a humbling task but one way or another I had to 'bounce back'.

I felt as though the song 'Eye of The Tiger' perfectly reflected my attitude and motivation. Here I was 'back on the street', or more accurately back on the doors, doing what I knew best – and doing it well.

I suppose, in retrospect, that at a very difficult time I reverted to what I knew and, as Trevor had kindly said, I was totally confident I could do the job.

Although I'd just spent nine months in jail, I'd added considerably to my armoury before that by taking up karate. I wasn't interested in passing the exams for my own personal reasons.

If you're a boxer, you can expect short shrift if you are caught up in a conflict that ends in court and I felt the same way about martial arts although ironically it did come back to haunt me when I got into trouble.

My main motivation was that I was very interested in improving my fitness and capacity to physically dominate people.

Instead of going to public classes, I had the benefit of private tuition with a very talented instructor, who was also a company director. Karate, as with all martial arts, emphasises self-discipline and poise rather than unbridled aggression and sheer force.

As a door supervisor, you need to have self defence skills. I did judo when I was very young. I was aged 18 to 19 when I used to perform my throws in the Wells Road club.

Then again 20 years later I found myself in a situation when I wanted to try something similar.

The first thing my instructor taught me was a kick in the chest. When I started, I could perform just 10 before giving it best. But two years of hard training later, it was more like 150.

Karate also shows you that the elbow is a very strong part of the anatomy.

I learnt a good many moves, or katas, as they are called. This discipline helps you to balance your body in preparation for a fight. I was good enough in the end to have been a black belt. Certainly if people crossed me, they'd be in big trouble.

The secret of martial arts is in the state of mind. Most people who are proficient at martial arts would not push things too far.

Everything is done with discipline and almost military precision. The mind and the body are working in unison.

Its main virtue is it teaches you not how to attack, but how to defend yourself. As a door supervisor, you are supposed to be a trained man and this certainly fits the bill.

Discipline often means achieving maximum results with the least necessary force, rather than the most.

If I could frighten someone without touching them at all, that is the most effective way of dealing with a troublesome situation. After all, that makes far more sense than actually hitting someone.

It is up to you to use all the tools at your disposal and that includes image and attitude more than the power of your fists.

It's difficult to put into words exactly what being proficient in martial arts does for you, but it certainly aided me to relax, keep my temper and react properly to situations.

Just as hard to define is the confidence it gives you to know that you've got something extra in your locker if you are put in a tight spot.

Perhaps it is best not to go into too much detail, but some of the most effective blows are a kick in the private parts, a punch to the side of the temple, a knee in the head and an elbow to the chest.

The beauty of this, if that's the right word, is that you can take someone out with a single action rather than caught in a slugging or wresting match.

I trained for a couple of years altogether and even got to learn how to run bare-footed, overcoming the initial pain.

I was dismayed, as I said before, when the issue of my being a martial arts man figured in the court case, but I was thoroughly delighted with the increased confidence and physical ability it provided me with.

I agreed to work for Trevor at The Royal for about £12 a night at a time when I desperately needed any money I could lay my hands on. Soon enough, more similar offers were flooding in, but that's another story.

Despite not being involved for a few years or so, I took to it again like a duck to water. I recognised the buzz of all the trouble associated with the job and needless to say the women were still looking at me.

I used to love watching them come into the various venues – dressed up, giggly, excited and out for a good time. People used to call me Sean Connery or Kenny Rogers.

So why I have I christened The Royal my 'Heartbreak Hotel' when I loved it, I still love it and I've had some fantastic times there. You see, I've always known, as in the words of that truly magnificent and soulful Elvis classic, that there's been something missing. I'll give you a clue, it begins with 'J' and ends in 'e'.

Just as the sparkle in a glass – the finest of champagnes perhaps excepted – is never quite matched by the satisfaction of the taste, the beauty, or otherwise, of the women could never match up to what I knew had been the real thing.

It's a very strange thing to try to explain to anyone else, but people who have experienced true and deep emotional pain will have a head start. Naturally physically I was still very attracted to the many women who often laid themselves purposely across my path in those days, yet inside I was tied completely in knots. Women were both God and The Devil, good and evil all at the same time to me. When it came to the crunch, I just couldn't face the possibility of getting hurt all over again.

It's going to be crazy tonight and I think I'm looking forward to it. There's a hen party in one of the bars and a group of businessmen in one of the restaurants. All mixing, in theory, with the weekend guests and other members of the public.

I've been to a thousand hen parties before, or at least I feel like I have. They are raucous, unpredictable affairs and, yes, there could just be some trouble. I'm always aiming to tread the tightrope just on the side of people enjoying themselves, but when it spills over into something more sinister, I've got to be there to catch them.

It's on my mind a lot on Friday when I'm going about my other work and it's on my mind as soon as I get home with just a couple of hours to go before my shift begins.

As I turn on the water of my refreshing shower, there's a familiar tightening feeling in my stomach. Anticipation, adrenalin, fear, all turned into one... It's a feeling I welcome and acknowledge. Without it, I simply couldn't be the same.

Then it's a case of putting on the battle armour – smart and neat enough to give the image of a man with just the right attention to detail and standards. Donning the traditional black suit always gives me a thrill. Suddenly all the other work of the day is forgotten and I'm becoming Don, the head doorman, again.

At the time, about 20 years ago, we had a very distinctive dress code. There was the white shirt, dicky bow and a black jacket.

Today it depends on what the particular management you are working for wants you to wear. But it usually includes a clip-on tie that makes it much harder for someone to grab you by the throat, and a smart jacket.

I get into my car and prepare to drive the familiar 15-minute journey into the heart of the city.

The Royal, or The Nottingham Royal Moathouse as it is known these days, is superbly located in the city centre just 50 yards from the Theatre Royal and Royal Centre complex.

Today it is an impressive city centre hotel with 210 bedrooms including crown executive rooms. It benefits from facilities including a 24-hour residents bar, two restaurants, a leisure club and 24-hour room service, not to mention its extensive meeting rooms.

Also these days Nottingham's new tram system gives guests access to the main railway station in under five minutes and helps make the hotel an even better choice for business and leisure guests.

At its height the massive complex would see between 4,500 and 5,000 people coming through the doors at a weekend. There could be 300 alone in The Penthouse and 250 in Grouchos, the next biggest bar.

If you, too, are Nottingham folk reading this and wonder why The Penthouse closed its doors a few years ago, I'm afraid I can't enlighten you too much. To be honest I think it was the biggest mistake the management there ever made.

Although obviously here I'm mentioning a few of the incidents that have needed my personal attention over the years, my personal highlight is in remembering that The Royal has always had an enviable record as regards its security.

I've worked for some great bosses over the years, but none better than Michael Sladell, who was general manager at both The Royal in Mansfield Road and in Wollaton Street for a spell of about six years in the late 1980s and early 1990s.

He took over the franchise for the hotel and did particularly well with it. A well educated and highly intelligent man, I particularly admired him for the fact that, although friendly and approachable, he was far from a push over. He knew exactly what he was doing.

I recall going into his office each Christmas and bringing him a bottle of champagne, or the like, as a gesture for all the work he'd put my way during the year. We would be there sipping a glass and I'd ask him if he was satisfied with what I'd been doing.

"Don," he answered. "If I wasn't satisfied, you wouldn't be here now." It's difficult to argue with that.

When I felt we needed to increase the wages, I'd get a similar positive response. He'd sit me down in his office and simply say: "Well, what do you want?" Then we'd thrash out the finer details and always come up with a deal.

A good looking bloke, who invariably kept his golden labrador in the office, Michael used to ask me to go with him as security when he went out to nightclubs. Again, in a more social setting, I found him to be a fantastic fellow and it was clear that we shared a mutual respect that is at the core of a really effective working relationship.

Michael is still in the hotel business, owning an establishment in Colchester, and I trust he is just as popular there.

Only just behind him in my view was a lady called Wendy Proctor, who was assistant manager during Michael's time as boss. Again she had an uncanny ability to deal with people, a feature that is so important in this line of work, and all in all was a terrific lady to work for. The place was a lot poorer without her when she moved on to a well-deserved promotion elsewhere.

Another fantastic guy was Brian Dunne. A genial Irishman, he always gave me a lot of support which was very important to have in my vulnerable line of work.

Although I can't mention them all by name, I've been very lucky with all the bosses I've worked under at The Royal. I honestly can't think of a bad one.

Naturally over the years there have been many famous guests staying at The Royal, particularly when they have been appearing over the road at the Theatre Royal.

My job obviously in such circumstances is to help ensure their trouble-free stay at the hotel rather than to engage them in fascinating conversation, but there have been some interesting moments.

The man I got the most time one-to-one with was that great Scottish comedian Billy Connelly. Maybe it was the Scottish ancestry in me, but I enjoyed a very lively 10 minutes or so with him one evening in The Penthouse.

There are some comedians who are not nearly so funny in the flesh, but I found Billy to be very sharp-witted and interesting to talk to.

I also shared common ground with the late Les Dawson, although I'm not sure he recognised me as a kindred spirit in the unusual circumstances in which we were introduced to each other.

Les, the host of Blankety Blank and the king of the mother-in-law jokes, was also a plumber by trade.

And this time his entrance to the hotel was certainly very comically timed. I'd been called to deal with this man who had been involved in a fight. He tried to hit me with a phone and even bit my arm. Anyway I had him in a head lock and bent over the reception desk when the big man walked in.

"Have I come to the right place?" he asked.

I also had the joy, if that's the right word, of keeping one of the era's great sex symbols from some of his enthusiastic admirers. David Essex was a top man with the ladies at the time and remains a superstar singer to this day.

Working at the time with my son Darryl, our task was to ensure that he had just the right number of ladies waiting for his autograph at any one time. We didn't want the poor man to get too overwhelmed.

Family Fortunes host Les Dennis must have also wondered whether someone was falling for him when my mate Rob, one of my top bouncers, fell over a table trying to video him. He made some suitably caustic remarks and took the mishap happily enough in his stride.

Another man who always had a reputation with the ladies was comedian Jim Davidson. His short stay with us was enlivened by a tiff with one of the staff, although what I will remember was the beautiful Bentley in the car park.

The incomparable Freddie Starr literally had me in stitches. He used his visit to perform an impromptu impression of being a bouncer. I don't know whether we learned anything more than he is certainly a great laugh.

On the other hand we got very little, except for the odd grunt, out of former world heavyweight boxing champion Frank Bruno. Perhaps he was missing his mate Harry.

Over the years there have been endless personalities staying with us. I'd be told of their stay in advance as a matter of policy. But, to be honest, I'm not really one of the star-struck variety, my job, as always, was to concentrate firmly on the demands of my job.

As I eased my way through the Nottingham city centre, I would be getting myself well and truly pumped up for the night ahead. Pulling into the car park and striding towards the entrance, I turned fully into the boss.

"Hello Don," chirps one of the doormen. I make a half-turn towards him and grunt a less audible greeting. The men need to know their place right from the start of the evening and that's not on chitty-chatty terms. Instead they need to pick up the vibes that I'm focused on my job.

There may be just a sprinkling of people inside the hotel compared with the hordes to come, but you don't wait for them to arrive to get to work.

I go on a tour of the building, ensuring that the fire escapes are clear, envisaging the number of guests that will be coming to each part of the hotel and finalising where I want my team.

I know exactly what the acceptable capacity is for each bar and restaurant and ensure my men are also on the ball. If there was to be a problem with the police or regarding the fire regulations, the buck would stop at me, so I need to know my business.

Many a night I've had men at the top and bottom of the stairs at The Penthouse in order to count the number of people already in and refuse others entry as a result.

Then I look round the toilets. These will be inspected on an hourly basis throughout the evening and are a key part of any venue. You really don't need me to tell you everything that goes on there.

Over the years I've seen some terrible sights in the toilets at The Royal. These have ranged from the more run-of-the-mill incidents with folk out of their minds from either drink or drugs, or very probably these days, both.

But the most appalling sights have been those of men literally queuing up to shag a young woman, probably bent over a wash basin with her skirt in the air. That type of young lady, who let's remember is some person's loved one, probably wakes up in the morning not even knowing who she has been with, or how many!

On several occasions I've seen young women pull up their skirts to expose their bare bottoms at me after they've just been thrown out. It's a highly regrettable symptom, no doubt, of the modern-day female transformation from lady to ladette.

Little wonder that we read of sexual diseases increasing in almost rampant fashion. It's frightening.

This is just one area in which women door supervisors come into their own. I may paint a predominantly macho picture of working on the doors – and physical brute force is certainly a factor – but it has been my privilege to work alongside talented female staff and I appreciate their worth from first-hand experience.

Dealing with people is a very complex art and women often have abilities that men lack. There are times also when it is far better that the member of staff is female for fairly obvious reasons.

Say we're bringing a woman or a group of women down in the lift to get them off the premises. You have to be very aware of the potential dangers in these circumstances, particularly as people want to get their own back on you.

The prospect of being accused of some form of sexual harassment is an ever-present worry, particularly these days.

I've had to deal with complaints about doormen myself, so I know how difficult it can be to discern one person's word against another.

But, having a woman as part of your team, means I can get an invaluable witness to what really went on.

I'm also far happier when there's a female available to attend to incidents in the women's toilets for fairly obvious reasons.

We have to be aware that toilets are places where tragedies could quite easily occur. That's why I insist on them being inspected at least hourly to ensure we haven't got guests in distress in there.

Altogether I've probably worked with about a dozen female bouncers or door supervisors and again, although I don't really want to name names, I've been genuinely impressed by all of them.

In my opinion it makes sound sense for any door team to have at least one member of the fairer gender.

Unlike with males, I don't think a woman's stature is that important here. We're not looking for butch women to compete with the males, but people with a certain presence and authority and that can come just as easily from a lady of much smaller physical build.

The lifts are a very important part of my check list. I need to know where we stand if we are going to have to get a drunk down from say The Penthouse on the eighth floor to the ground floor to get them out of the building.

We've had many a problem along the way in the past, as you can imagine with people struggling and brawling in the lift. This has caused the lift to jam on several occasions, giving us anxious moments as we radio for help.

I also had one nightmare when there was a bomb alert in the lift and we faced the awkward dilemma of whether to evacuate the whole hotel. Police were called and diffused the possible emergency by stopping the lift and looking underneath, where such a device would have been placed.

Needless to say in such sensitive times we have been well versed in the procedures to undertake if there was to be a serious bomb threat. But perhaps it is not wise to go down that road here.

My doormen are giving off a mixture of non-verbal messages. Some look a little pensive, even tired, others are mentally preening themselves for the arrival of all the customers, particularly the young women!

People are attracted to the doors because of the glamour. I know because I've been there, done it and enjoyed the benefits. We're smartly dressed, authority figures that women tend to look up to.

Particularly these days when people tend to dress down and casual rather than smart and sharp, the doorman tends to stand out. Also there's something in the perceived sense of power that makes him an obvious target for the ladies.

But, without neglecting the social side, the really good bouncer, or door supervisor, as they are termed today is more like a professional soccer referee. They say the best officials are those you barely notice and that's the way I operate too.

Our job is to go about our business quietly and efficiently, not to take centre stage and be the highlight of the evening's entertainment. In effect, the fewer times we are called into direct action, the better we are doing our jobs. Contrary to what most people might think, most door supervisors are far happier when they are able to go home without being involved in a brutal confrontation.

As the night gets under way, I'll make a series of mini-tours. If I'm doing nothing, it's not because there is nothing going, it's because I'm missing something.

Even as I enter each room my training is playing a major role in what I do. I'll stand in positions where I have a particularly good view of everyone and everything that is happening and where I am less of a physical target.

I take mental notes on anyone who catches my attention. It takes a professional eye to spot them, but potential problem-causers stick out a mile to me.

When working at venues with dance floors you have to be extremely well organised. These are places where a great many people are inevitably in very close proximity, so the potential for flashpoints is very high.

The typical incident in which someone takes offence at another bloke looking at his girlfriend can quickly escalate into an all-out fight involving 20 or 30 people.

My men need to be there to identify trouble almost at its source, working in co-operation with the DJ. The usual procedure is stop the music, put on the lights and we go straight in and get rid of the offenders. Once they are off the premises, the vast majority can then get on with enjoying the evening.

Very often the job is done so quickly and efficiently that guests are unaware just what has happened. On many occasions I've had guests come up to me and say; "What's happened to my mate, I just went to the toilet and he's gone."

"He wasn't feeling well and had to go home," I answer.

The first principle of the job is that you don't want trouble in your venue. Therefore as prevention is a far more healthy alternative than cure, we need to be very careful whom we let in.

Confronting a situation at source may seem difficult at the time, but it's far easier than trying to sort it out half-a-dozen pints later.

I see some lads scruffily dressed, singing raucously and heading roughly in the direction of The Royal. Already I know that they don't really belong here, it's just the next bar on their crawl.

"Sorry you're not coming in lads!" I say. Now is the crucial time waiting for their reaction. There's two main possibilities. Either they will question my authority, mutter some oaths and swear to get their revenge on me – they're the ones who aren't coming in next week, the week after that or any time at all for that matter. Or there's the good-natured folk who might be genuinely disappointed, but keep their emotions in order.

"Come back next week, lads, and you'll be all right," I say. "Thanks mate!" they reply. A potentially difficult situation has been quickly diffused.

It sounds selfish to suggest that once the source of the trouble is off our doorstep that's the end of the matter, but that's largely true.

Once someone is back on the streets, he or she is the responsibility of the police.

The relationship between doormen and the police is crucial to a doorman's job and, in my experience, this has proved more often than not to be excellent.

The police simply could not do their job without us – and they realise as much. In Nottingham there are about 20 police officers working the night shift at any one time and when you consider the sheer numbers of people in the pubs, bars and clubs, you can soon appreciate how the odds are stacked against them.

The police often take a real hammering both from the public and from the media. But, as far as I'm concerned, they do a brilliant job. Their discipline and patience under the utmost provocation is often amazing. And, let's remember they are not super human, they are just mere human beings, like the rest of us.

They don't have the option of handing responsibility over to someone else however vile the behaviour they are subjected to. Maybe they have to take the offenders to hospital to be treated, before carting them off to the police station as they continue to aim verbal and physical abuse in their direction.

It can't be a very pleasant thought.

When people speak to me about the weaknesses of the police I cringe because without them we'd all be in one hell of an unholy mess.

The job has changed a great deal over the years. There was nowhere near as many people wanting to be bouncers when I went back to The Royal, yet now there are about 2,000 doormen in the city of Nottingham alone. Unlike the days when I first started, you have to have a badge to do the job and this has some advantages and some disadvantages.

I've always considered myself to be a natural on the doors. Put simply, God has either given you it, or he hasn't.

To me, someone who is about 5'6" tall and about 10 to 12 stones dripping wet has big problems to start with. You need a bit of power and image is also very important. If you look big and look the part, that's half the battle as far as many potential trouble-causers is concerned.

But, on the other hand, if they fancy their chances against you just on account of your physical appearance and bearing then you're going to find yourself in more battles than you are going to want to handle.

One night we were presented with the difficult prospect of a full-scale altercation between groups of lads from London and Birmingham in the top bar.

The management had already had to call the police once during the evening which proved a very traumatic one for the staff.

It was certainly a night to forget for the manager at the time, a lovely lady called Linda, who was attacked by one of the unruly youths. I was quickly on the scene to give him a whack in his private parts and I grabbed another coward, who started to whimper as though he was going to burst into tears.

At one stage both Denis and I were grappling with three or four each and all in all it was a contest between around 40 men and seven bouncers.

Fortunately after a while we managed to calm things down although the door staff had to stay until the early hours of the morning to ensure everyone's safety.

The problem with hotels, compared certainly to pubs, clubs and restaurants, is that you get domestic incidents.

A woman made a complaint to me that this guy had been trying to entice her into his room. We went up to his room with the manager and he made things worse by pulling the manager through the door.

I ordered him to let him go and then gave him a piece of quick retribution by kneeing him in his private parts.

He was eventually given two choices by the police – either to stay in his room and keep out of trouble or be kicked out. Happily he chose the former.

We're not talking about hotel problems here or anything that is inherently associated with The Royal and The Royal alone. We're talking about a society problem whereby when people have a drink or two they kick off.

Hotels are a lot harder to run than the pubs. This is because of the wider responsibilities involved. In a pub or nightclub, you are getting people straight out onto the streets and on their way, but when you are dealing with guests in restaurants and bars you need to be more diplomatic because ultimately you are responsible to the management of the hotel.

Virtually anyone could spot some violence in a pub and throw someone out the door, but it's a different skill entirely to go into a restaurant, cool an inflamed situation down and ensure everything is sorted out without having to resort to the police.

Hotel guests don't want to see blue flashing lights every five minutes. They will begin to wonder just what sort of place they are staying at. If they see trouble, it is very likely they may well decide never to stay at the hotel again, whereas trouble in a pub is perhaps more predictable.

Responsibilities are far wider. For example, I've always had a very large multi-storey car park to police which is a major task in itself. We're not just talking about keeping things under control in the hotel building, because if one of the guests suffers damage to his or her vehicle that has also ruined the stay completely. So I've always sub-contacted work to car park attendants or put my own men on patrol there when this has not proved possible.

I have run one of the biggest hotels for 20 years and I have never had the police on my back. We've never had problems that we couldn't handle ourselves.

If you've ever watched those legendary Carry On films, you'll appreciate one particular incident that occurred in The Penthouse a few years ago. Needless to say, however, the humour was only apparent in retrospect for at the centre of the action was neither Hattie Jacques, nor Barbara Windsor for that matter, but a woman who was obviously in a world of her own. We were working upstairs when we got a call that this woman was in the hotel wearing just a white coat with absolutely nothing underneath. She was pretending, it seems, to be a doctor!

She had been moving from floor to floor attracting a good few admiring looks no doubt, but also a fair few complaints.

My first action was to get the duty manager because in these circumstances a doorman on his own can be very vulnerable and my caution was fully justified.

She accused both the manager, then a police officer of trying to rape her. Eventually the woman, who appeared to be in her 40s and wasn't particularly the worse for alcohol, was led away, presumably to have more than her medical credentials examined!

There was also more than an element of farce about events at an Irish wedding. We've all heard of the phrase "biting your head off", but on this occasion one of the guests had bitten off another person's ear! Then as a doorman rushed in to rescue it, one of the female guests had bent down and run off with the poor bloke's ear.

Anyway she was soon restrained and, as far as I'm aware, normal hearing was resumed after the prompt attention of Nottingham hospital staff.

Never believe, however, that you are totally indispensable. As soon as you do, circumstances will prove you wrong.

We had all finished our shift and were up in The Penthouse relaxing when we were alerted to a fight in the banqueting suite down below. Four doormen immediately got into the lift ready for action. The only problem was that a good 90 minutes later we were still there!

The lift used to have its unpredictable moments and this was one of the less timely of them all.

By the time we were released from our 'cage', the people down below had sorted the situation out themselves!

Another occasion when the lift got stuck was a little more serious. To be honest, there wasn't a lot wrong with the lift, it was more usually a case of too many drunken guests wrecking the mechanism.

You may wonder why you see notices on the outside of lifts stating how many people it can safely transport.

Such logic, however, often used to go out of the window at such a hectic place at The Royal when the lift was in almost constant use and guests were picking it up over a number of floors.

Problems were caused both by the number of people on board and when the more drunken ones decided to bounce up and down on the journey.

The usual sticking point was between the sixth and fifth floors and that's exactly what happened one night when a group of guys and girls, who'd clearly enjoyed themselves during the evening, went for a ride.

One girl, in particular, was going hysterical. She not only suffered from claustrophobia, a condition with which I could easily sympathise, but the stress was also bringing on an asthma attack.

We had to go to the top of the building and wind the lift back up, quite a physical task. Then I treated the woman, giving her an inhaler and trying to keep her calm. We considered calling the medics but in the end she was all right to continue her revelry unaided.

They say it's best to be safe rather than sorry, but we had to laugh one night when one of our doormen got a bit too cautious. Spotting a man on the roof, he immediately closed down the festivities and called the fire brigade.

Little did he know but it was nothing more suspicious than one of the electricians going about his work. Imagine his surprise when he was suddenly confronted by the screaming sound of five fire engines arriving. Never mind, at least the bloke was trying to do the right thing.

A much more real alarm occurred when some bright spark decided he wanted to burn the hotel down. He went up into one of the toilets and set a fire there.

The incident was safely diffused and he didn't realise that we had a fair idea who had done it. Next time he came into the hotel Michael Sladell alerted me and the police were called. He started to get clever with the two officers and I grabbed him and told him to shut up.

Talking about being clever, I had to – grudgingly – admire the cheek of a DJ one night in Grouchos. It was time the party stopped, so I went down and told him that he could play just one more record and that would be it.

Half an hour later I went back into the bar and the music was still in full flow.

"I thought I told you just one more record," I said.

"Yes, mate, it's an LP," he replied.

The behaviour of women sometimes almost takes your breath away – and not for the right reasons.

One notable incident occurred in one of our plush restaurants when three girls took offence at a middle aged couple on the next table

We were called because the argument had evolved into a fight and I quickly isolated the main female ring leader.

I told her she would have to leave and she immediately launched into a stream of expletives.

"I am going to cut your heart out and eat it," she shouted. Very appetising stuff, I'm sure you'd agree, in front of all the dinner guests.

She continued by trying to get her shoes off to whack me with and also attempting to head-butt and kick me.

I was having so much trouble calming her down I threatened to throw her down the stairs to get her out of the way.

When we finally showed her the exit door, she responded in typical style by baring her bottom at us.

Then she started throwing bottles, the police were called and she ended up getting herself arrested.

Now I'm a man who can turn the air blue like the rest of them, but her language that night was almost enough to make a doorman blush!

I also got to see a different side of a caring profession when a girl got glassed at a private function.

The victim was in a right mess with blood going everywhere meanwhile this generously-proportioned woman was ranting and raving about wanting to kill me and everyone around her.

It took three police officers between 10 and 15 minutes just to get her into the car! I was less than impressed when I found out that she was a nurse, although that's no general comment on what is a very commendable vocation.

A Christmas event at The Royal certainly went with a swing. Firstly, we had a particularly good band on and they certainly got the guests into a party spirit.

Problem was it was more like a chimp's tea party. It kicked off with people throwing food around and old Scrooge himself – that's me – told them that if there was going to be any more fooling around, I'd close the whole show down. Denis, too, was on the prowl and not too many people muck with him.

But there was no stopping one particular woman who clambered up onto a table and started swinging by the chandaliers!

Her Tarzan impression finally fell when she came crashing down to earth. The chandelier not surprisingly gave way and she fell onto a table knocking food and bottles all over the place.

I encountered one of the more durable characters to cause trouble at The Royal when I got a radio message and saw big Ken holding this guy in an arm lock with blood coming out of his head.

The guy was on the floor and when I lifted him up he was in a bloody mess!

However he surprised us when the police came. An officer was in the process of handcuffing him when he punched the officer onto the floor.

This time I put my knee to his throat, virtually winding him and making it easier for the officer to get the cuffs on.

The violence continued when the bloke, who didn't look particularly beefy, assaulted one of the hospital staff. He was given short shrift by the law when he came to court.

In no way, whatsoever, am I trying to give the impression that The Royal has been anything but well run by relating all these incidents.

To gain a sense of proportion you have to look at it two ways. Firstly, I've worked at the place for a very long time and the numbers of people who have come through our doors are virtually uncountable during that time.

The Royal has been, for much of that time, one of Nottingham's top social venues – the place to see and be seen – rather than a typical hotel where non-residents might wonder if they were welcome.

In all honesty I've discovered that it doesn't matter whether people are in the most downmarket of pubs or the plushest of hotels when one ingredient is present.

Alcohol affects the behaviour of all types of people beyond all recognition and I always expected to tackle at least one fight during a typical weekend shift.

I probably know more about the Royal hotel than even the manager – and that's not showing any disrespect – where the security side is concerned.

The young gun slinger might want to gain a reputation, the old gun slinger doesn't need to impress people, but just goes about his business knowing that the more time the gun stays in his holster the better for everyone.

Learning how to deal with people is one of a doorman's prime skills. The clever doorman is one who can get someone to do what he or she wants without using any physical force.

When you're a doorman you can never fully be off duty. One night we were sitting relaxing at about 2.30am well after the end of our shift when the call went out that about a dozen folk were causing trouble in the banqueting suite.

I grabbed this bloke in a head lock, only for one of his mates to smack me on the side of the head and smash me straight down on a glass top table. "What are you doing down there, boss?" mused Denis as he surveyed the unusual scene.

Nevertheless Denis and co helped us to get all the trouble makers out and finish the night on top. Denis the menace put a shirt over the troublemaker concerned and gave him a bit of his own medicine.

One feature of a hotel life is domestic arguments. On one occasion when I was working with Jackie Wright, a former policewoman, we had to deal with an incident when a man claimed someone else was making passes at his partner.

The boyfriend had then hit the other man and started a brawl.

Later on that evening there was more trouble and we called up to the couple's room.

Jackie told the bloke to get out, but the woman wanted to go with him. I went up into the room, grabbed the bloke and dragged him downstairs whilst Jackie came down with the girlfriend.

The incident ended with the bloke driving out of the car park in a drunken state and duly being picked up further down the road by the police. I suppose it just wasn't his day and I certainly didn't get an invite to a future wedding!

I had a special party to celebrate my 50th birthday party in The Penthouse and people came from all over the country to celebrate with me.

They called me The Godfather or Big Man. I was 16-stones and still very much looked the part. My hair was grey and I had a full beard, I was often likened to the famous folk singer Kenny Rogers and it was something I quite enjoyed hearing.

There were naturally problems caused by my getting ever older. Some people would start taking the mickey and, although I'd never allow them the satisfaction of thinking they were getting at me, secretly it hurt more than just a little.

When you've been a man, who has taken pride in his appearance and been rightly recognised as a genuine tough guy, it is very hard to take some youngster, whom I'd gladly take over my knee and give a good spanking,

Not so long ago I was in The Royal when I had to reprimand a young bloke, probably about three times as young as me.

"What are you going to do about it, Santa Claus?" he chirped, no doubt thinking he was very funny.

I went over to him, grabbed him by his trendy ponytail and banged his head down hard against the table where he and his friends were sitting.

"All right, mate, I don't want any trouble," he gasped, sounding just as pathetic as my view of him.

Young, fit and relatively able he might have been, but I could still eat people like him for breakfast. His bad luck was picking on the wrong soon-to-be pensioner!

Invariably these sort of lads want to get the last word in order to save face. They'll point pretend guns at you, mouth obscenities and, usually from a distance, shout about what they're going to do to you when they return.

Usually I will just ignore them, to be honest they are too pathetic to be worthy of my attention, but occasionally I will put them into place.

I'll tell the would-be assassins; "Come on, then, do it right now. But, if you don't do a good job and kill me, I'll get up in the morning and come and bury you!" That tends to shut them up although I do admit that these days with so many people on drugs, it does cross my mind that someone could actually be crazy enough to carry out such a gun threat. That's the world we are now living in.

Only about four years ago I was going home in my Volvo estate and was in Parliament Street. When I got to the traffic lights, this group of lads gave chase and I soon realised who they were. I'd just banned them from The Royal and they'd come to get revenge.

It was about 3am and in that circumstance you've got no-one to help you. I just put my foot down and made my escape. Live to fight another day, that's my motto.

I am quite an easy person to identify physically and there have been endless times when I've been out socially and have overheard folk saying: "Look, there's that doorman from The Royal."

You are basically a sitting target. That's why I do not use my name around here. A lot of people near where I live call me Mr Black.

If someone asked for a Mr McCalman, most would say quite rightly that they'd never heard the name, and BT would also deny any knowledge either of the name either.

A friend of Wally Waldron once told me there was a contract out on me from a doorman in Clifton. I was told the same thing again by my mate Trevor Austin.

But it never unduly worried me and I'd still do my job exactly the same way as though nothing happened.

My attitude is that there's never any point in worrying about things that, almost certainly, will never happen. If I had a fiver for every time I've received a threatening phone call, for example, I'd probably own BT let alone provide it with so much of its advertising!

I am, as I've said, very security conscious. So I just continue to do the right thing and leave the rest to trust.

I've always been an authority figure and that fits well with an image of a doorman. We stick out in the crowd. Women look at you and they feel reassured.

Women want to be on the right side of you. They are attracted to doormen.

You are easily identifiable at a function because of your dress. There you are in a nice dinner suit with a butterfly collar and a dicky bow and a lot of the men are wearing jeans. You've got a definite head start.

Women, generally, like a smart man and they like the tough guy image too.

Right until my 60th birthday I worked very regularly on the doors in the Nottingham area.

I loved the life, the power, and the authority that went with it. There was the joy of having women flock up to you and the simply indescribable feel of marching down a room, flanked by men in whom I'd trust my very life, to sort out a potentially dangerous situation.

There was the time when after a satisfying and eventful night on the doors, we'd all go out clubbing in the city centre.

Still buzzing from the thrill of a job well done, I'd walk into a club, surrounded by friends, and be recognised straightaway.

There would be drinks, attention from lovely-looking women and a guaranteed good time.

There was the respect from fellow doormen who always looked up at me with a kind of healthy awe, whether they had been in my personal good books that night or not.

With the role of a doorman comes a certain aura and it was that, I think, that gave me the confidence to chat up women and play the part.

One classic dilemma is that of reasonable force. You are allowed, the law says, to use reasonable force. But what does that mean? Does it mean the same thing in very different situations?

For example, if someone has got a knife and is threatening to stab me, what constitutes a lawful response?

One of the most highly publicised incidents where this became an issue outside of the doors was that of the farmer Tony Martin, who shot a burglar.

I do have a great deal of sympathy with his plight – he was, as we all know, sent to prison, but he made the mistake of continuing to act when the raider was leaving his property.

That is where the door supervisor has to draw the line and I would suggest the average householder, trying to protect his or her property, does the same thing too. I feel that if someone is coming at you with a bottle, for example, you have a perfect right to disable them in such a way as they are unable to use it. You can't afford to pussy foot around in such dangerous circumstances.

The first point is that you have to defend yourself and ensure that you live another day.

This could involve striking someone and using a degree of violence, but it should only be done on your property.

I am always prepared for anyone who tries to break into my house. I live a very secluded life and it would be easy to identify someone who has no right to be here.

Let's put it this way, if anyone tried to attack anyone of my family, they would whatever the law says, lose the right to live in my opinion.

In my career I have encountered virtually every situation you could imagine on the doors

Being a professional doorman and vice chairman of the Door Watch Committee means I have to be very careful how I deal with situations in everyday life.

For example, if I see a woman broken down at the side of the motorway, my first instinct might be to stop, but that could well be the wrong thing to do.

Imagine what might happen to that woman and could I be implicated in some way?

No, it is far better to use your mobile phone and call the police or other emergency services to come to her assistance.

Despite all this, it is the happy memories, such as the very special parties I had for my 50th and 60th birthdays and sharing Christmas as I invariably did with my doormen in The Penthouse, that have helped to counter-balance the sadness of my Heartbreak Hotel.

Just read the words at the end of this chapter that still have pride of place on my wall at home...

Although I still go to The Royal each Saturday evening to pay the lads, it hurts that I'm no longer quite as well recognised as I once was.

But, yes, I admit that I miss The Royal more than perhaps I have previously dared to admit. It will always have a very special place in my heart and remain, in my view, a venue of which Nottingham should be justly proud.

My experience of The Royal speaks to me so much about how fate takes a distinct hand in our lives. If my domestic life had turned out as I wanted it to, I would never again have covered the doors and fallen for my 'Heartbreak Hotel'.

Yet by doing so, I've become a very well known Nottingham character and done a job that I know I can be proud of.

Truly my experience at The Royal has been full of agony and esctasy. Perhaps it is not possible to hit your personal heights in life without 'going through The Mill'.

HEARTBREAK HOTEL

Well, since my baby left me,
I found a new place to dwell.
It's down at the end of lonely street
At heartbreak hotel.
You make me so lonely baby,
I get so lonely,
I get so lonely I could die.
And although it's always crowded,
You still can find some room.
Where broken hearted lovers
Do cry away their gloom.
You make me so lonely baby,
I get so lonely,
I get so lonely I could die.
Well, the bell hop's tears keep flowin',
And the desk clerk's dressed in black.
Well they been so long on lonely street
They ain't ever gonna look back.
You make me so lonely baby,
I get so lonely,
I get so lonely I could die.
Hey now, if your baby leaves you,
And you got a tale to tell.
Just take a walk down lonely street
To heartbreak hotel.

I

SURVIVOR – EYE OF THE TIGER

Risin' up, back on the street
Did my time, took my chances
Went the distance, now I'm back on my feet
Just a man and his will to survive
So many times, it happens too fast
You change your passion for glory
Don't lose your grip on the dreams of the past
You must fight just to keep them alive
Chorus:
It's the eye of the tiger, it's the cream of the fight
Risin' up to the challenge of our rival
And the last known survivor stalks his prey in the night
And he's watchin' us all in the eye of the tiger
Face to face, out in the heat
Hangin' tough, stayin' hungry
They stack the odds 'til we take to the street
For we kill with the skill to survive
chorus
Risin' up, straight to the top
Have the guts, got the glory
Went the distance, now I'm not gonna stop
Just a man and his will to survive
chorus
The eye of the tiger (repeats out)...

MOAT
HOUSE

NOTTINGHAM
ROYAL

5th December 1999

<u>**TO WHOM IT MAY CONCERN**</u>

<u>**MR. DON McCALMAN**</u>
<u>**DON McCALMAN SECURITIES**</u>

Don McCalman and his team have worked at The Nottingham Royal Moat House for nearly 16 years looking after security for the hotel and its guests, on a daily basis and also assisting with large functions.

He has always proved to be reliable, trustworthy and pleasant with our residents, guests and staff, and I would not hesitate in recommending him to other companies who are seeking a security company on a similar basis.

Yours Faithfully

Graham Sheperd,
GENERAL MANAGER

Chapter 7

Door to Door

WORD soon spread about my new-found reputation from working at The Royal Hotel and I was quickly inundated with security requests.

At our height McCalman Securities had as many as 50 men working on any one night when we were also covering the likes of The Ossington Hotel, Blue Bell, Mint Bar, George Hotel, Red Lion at Retford and even a bar in Doncaster. That was all as recently as about ten years ago.

When I started to get into my mid-50s, I no longer wanted to be running all over Nottingham and beyond sorting out the pubs and doors, so I started to cut down.

At one stage I was regularly making the 30-minute journey to Newark, a place I found had more than its fair share of problems.

One of the DJs at the Ossington Hotel recommended that I should be called in after the number of incidents in the fun bar began to get out of hand. I certainly encountered enough trouble of my own.

I initially went down there with a lad called Rob, one of my tried and trusted doormen, although he eventually got more than he'd bargained for.

At the back of the hotel was a bar with a large disco area with steps down to the River Trent.

There were incidents virtually every weekend. Newark at the time had a lot of travelling people and gangs. I would get threats of being shot whilst attacks with bottles and fights were pretty commonplace. I probably had a couple of dozen direct death threats during my spell there.

The most serious problem of all came after about 18 months. Rob got involved in a fight when some lads had had a go at him and ended up wading in and putting this thug well and truly in his place. He finished with cuts to his face and his shirt in tatters.

Problem was he was part of a gang and they made it clear they wanted revenge. They were asking where Rob lived as they wanted to even things up. They knew by that time that our door company was from Nottingham and even started to ask folk round the city too.

If they didn't find out Rob's whereabouts, they'd wreck the place. Didn't sound like a very good deal to me, but we needed to take notice.

Even the manager of the Ossington was worried because rumours of what was about to happen were spreading fast and he wanted to know just what was going on. I reassured him that I would be there to deal with it personally and the safety of everyone there would naturally be my main priority.

The obvious course of action was to ensure Rob wasn't on duty on the Sunday night when they'd vowed to return. I met up with my team in Nottingham that night and told them that I'd be on the case before we made our 30-minute trip to Newark.

I was waiting in exactly the right spot when the gang leader, who was accompanied by about 12 mates, made his appearance. I was standing on the steps above him and was therefore in an advantageous position if he'd tried to fight there and then.

He asked where Rob was and again made his intentions clear, so I told him: "You are not coming in!". "Who is going to stop me then?" he said. "I am!"

He threatened me that he'd take me out and started to get very cocky, so I went on the attack. I told him that he'd better do a good job because I'd come back for him and settle everything once and for all.

The main protagonist threatened that, as they knew we were from Nottingham, they'd be waiting on the A46 that night ready to shoot us.

As you can imagine it was a fairly wary lot of doormen who drove out of Newark that night, but there was no sign of any suspicious vehicles on the A46, so we lived to fight another day.

They kept coming back week after week and the answer was always the same. They were barred because of the threats they had made against my staff and I wasn't for turning. I told them they were welcome to keep coming back any night they wanted, but the answer would always be the same.

If I'd run 10 places in Newark at the time, they wouldn't have got a sniff at any of them.

The group turned up at The Daisy Club across the road. I ran this door, too, and we kept in close touch about potential troublemakers like these. This was an absolutely prime example of my point that the most obvious way you can prevent trouble is at the door itself by not letting folk inside in the first place.

Otherwise there would have been real problems for both my staff and the other guests and it could have got really nasty. Mind you, they'd never have found Rob in there. I transferred him to another door and he wasn't seen in Newark again. It was best, I felt, to take as much aggravation out of a difficult situation as possible and so it proved.

I had a two-year contract at the Ossington and worked on there for a shorter spell afterwards and also did a couple of years at the Daisy Club, which was basically a late night drinking den.

The Daisy Club was a Friday and Saturday night job which meant that I'd usually be leading my men from Nottingham as The Royal and the pubs and clubs there were my main job. But, if they had a function on, I'd make sure I went there personally in my red XJS and ensured everything was in order. All things being equal I'd be back at The Royal by about 10pm.

There was trouble there and it was our job to ensure that the gangs couldn't rule the roost. Our priority were the ordinary folk who just wanted a quiet drink and that meant the trouble stayed outside as much as possible.

I enjoyed my time at the Ossington although I was grateful that I'd insisted on a contract. The management tried to go back on the deal, but I told them the agreement was legally binding and that I'd be staying.

It all ended in tears in Newark though as the new management let me down big style. I still had two men out there each Friday and Saturday evening for another year after the end of the contract but there were financial problems. In the end they owed me about £2,000 by the time the new management went bankrupt.

It was time to kiss goodbye to Newark and all its problems. It was no great problem for me as the bulk of my work remained, as always, back home in Nottingham.

Have you ever watched one of those glorious Westerns where the hero of the piece takes out all his enemies in one fell swoop, almost without breaking sweat? Not real life is it? But one night at The Mint Bar in Friar Lane, Nottingham, the regulars witnessed a scene that would keep them talking for years.

With the owner off one evening, I clocked in to ensure everything was all right. I asked these lads to leave as they were being rowdy, but they didn't want to go without a fight.

I smacked the first lad and he hit the deck, but another potential bruiser came right up behind me. Instinctively I stuck out an elbow fair and square in his face to give him a nasty nose and eye job.

Almost instantaneously, it was third time lucky. I brought my leg up and gave this other lad a fearful crack as he fell down to his knees.

The whole incident took just seconds and would have looked corny if it had been choreographed.

The whole place went quiet, apart from a few nervous references to me, as I shut the door. I walked back knowing everyone was staring at me.

I gave no bodily indication of my feelings as though such work was a boringly regular occurrence. But inside I was shaking like a leaf. I realised well enough that but for the grace of God that night, I would have been the one nursing serious wounds in both body and pride.

It was just a case of everything working perfectly and a fair bit of luck thrown in!

At Michael Isaacs, a club in Huntingdon Street, I was plunged head first into a battle between the previous team of bouncers and the bosses. I went down there with a lad called Lance and I knew we would get some trouble. Soon enough a bloke confronted me and warned: "If I were you, mate, I wouldn't work here again."

"Do you know who I am?" I replied. He promised he'd be back to sort us out the next day.

As we were working that night, we were fully aware that they were waiting for us across the road. So as I drove my XJS into Parliament Street, I wasn't too surprised to discover there were two cars following me. I raced across the red lights to put some distance between us.

I ended up parking my car in nearby Gregory Street and clambering over a fence to scramble into my home. I waited for some time to see if they'd managed to track me, but I'd successfully given them the slip.

You can appreciate better from such incidents why I am reluctant even to reveal my name or where I live. There's always the prospect of some nutter trying to take his retribution home and coming to get me.

I've lived with so many threats, they are almost water off a duck's back. But it doesn't mean that I haven't been vigilant. Why do you think I live as a semi-recluse with cameras and other security and most people near where I live don't even know me by my correct surname? It always pays to be one step ahead.

I'd check Libertys, a nearby nightclub door we used to cover, The Blue Bell and The George and ring the lads in Newark and aim to be back at The Royal for about 11pm. At each of the venues I'd be very cordially greeted and know everyone.

I ran The George Hotel on the corner of George Street for 14 years heading a team of four doormen. This was a place where there was always plenty of trouble, but happy memories too including Mary working behind the bar with her beehive haircut. She was a true character of her time and so well liked that we were all so upset when she finally called time.

There was always plenty for the doormen to get their teeth into as you would expect from a venue in the heart of the Lace Market.

Mind you, all of us were taken aback one night when a massive fight kicked off and we eventually had to shut the doors completely. The offenders threatened that they'd be back the next night, too, and this was one threat we had to take seriously.

Twenty hours later we were reinforced by a dozen more doormen from Leicester. They were stationed outside the hotel waiting for the thugs who never showed. It was a case, however, of better safe than sorry and I wasn't going to put my usual loyal staff to undue risk.

Another night I got involved in a rumpus with a lad who tried to attack me with a bottle. I managed to wrestle him to the floor and he subsequently got arrested. Job done.

There were the usual round of death threats and I got kicked and spat at, which is something I particularly detest. Out of all the variations of disgusting human behaviour this is very near the top and one of the most humiliating to be on the receiving end of.

Denis had his car smashed whilst we were there, reinforcing my idea that it was usually better to go into town by taxi. One of the first ways the thugs look to get at you is if they know your vehicle, so I didn't want to give them that opportunity

When you're running the doors you just had to expect this. It never worried me and there wasn't the slightest chance that I'd give way. It's the same with death threats and even the talk of contracts being taken out on you. What's the point in getting all steamed up? I just take all the necessary precautions and leave it at that.

If you get too worried about such stuff, you probably shouldn't be doing the doors in the first place.

The worst incident at this particular bar was when a really bad fight flared up in the toilets. A bloke tried to hit me, but I grabbed him and pushed him away down the stairs. It was an incident that merited a report in the Evening Post.

I was at the George Hotel one Saturday night at about 9pm when I saw these lads, whom I didn't like the look of, coming up to the door. I was at the door with three other doormen.

"I know Chris Bailey!" said one clever dick. Now I've got plenty of time for Chris myself, but that wasn't the point.

"I don't care who you know, you're not coming in," I said.

One of the lads tried to kick me, so I grabbed his leg and he went straight to the floor.

I asked again: "Are you going to behave?" but the youth continued to struggle and then grabbed a bottle and hurled it through the window. I chased after him and tripped him up, telling him bluntly that he'd just landed himself a big bill to pay for a new window.

The next week he was back with a gang of four or five mates in tow. "Remember me?" he said.

"You got me into loads of trouble!" "You better go now!" I replied. "Otherwise I'm going to give you a real hiding.

It was then that one of his friends recognised me. "Sorry, mate, I didn't realise it was you," he said, leading a retreat of the young man's followers.

He was on his own again when I warned him: "If I ever see you again, I'm going to bury you!" I'd also been to The George one night when Mick contacted me on his walkie-talkie to ask me to go down to The Blue Bell.

"There are some youths drinking very heavily in here and they're beginning to get a bit funny," he said.

Thelma behind the bar has also picked up the vibes and asked me to have a word with the lads. There were about 10 of them altogether, a serious looking equation when you think there were only two of us."

I said: "Calm down, you're getting a bit rowdy."

"All right, mate," was the reasonable enough reply.

But as I was walking out, I heard another one say: "F--- off".

"I want you out now," I replied. "Who is going to make us," he said.

"If you don't, I can have 10 doormen here within five minutes. It's up to you – you either go the easy way or the hard way."

The threats continued, but again my reputation got me out of what could have been a very tight corner.

"I know you, you're from The Royal and your name is Don," said this lad.

"Sorry about the trouble, we'll go now."

This was really the reverse of the old adage that one bad apple spoils the whole bunch. In this case one decent lad came to the rescue and played a major role in ensuring that the situation didn't get any further out of hand.

What people don't realise sometimes in these circumstances is that once you have taken your stand, there's no hiding place.

Once I'd gone in there and told them to leave, I couldn't possibly have backed down or I would have lost all respect, not least my self respect.

It is probably only afterwards that you realise how close you were to getting very seriously hurt.

The numbers were loaded very much against us on this occasion and it was my threat to bring in more doormen that made them think again.

Doormen of mine faced an unusual temptation at an Irish wedding with around 100 guests at the Gateway Hotel in Cinder Hill.

We had four doormen who unwittingly got caught in the middle of a fight. One set of guests said they'd pay the doormen £500 for each of the other gang they beat up.

When the doormen wisely turned the invitation down, the guests turned on them. The doormen, who again on this occasion were hopelessly outnumbered, ran for their lives and when I arrived police were on the scene, but the rest of the security presence had all gone.

When I went in to try to calm the situation down I was completely on my own.

But, fortunately, I knew quite a lot of the older folk at the wedding and this helped me in my cause. They said it was the younger ones who had kicked off and were basically on my side.

The next day when I got to speak with my doormen again they explained they'd left because they feared they would be kicked to hell.

To be honest I think their judgment was right, but luckily so was mine in backing myself to be able to sort it all out.

I got even closer to the long arm of the press through my five months working at The Blue Bell in Parliament Street only five minutes from The Royal. The reason was that at the time the crime reporter for the local paper was dating the daughter of the landlord and landlady Jeff and Thelma, a nice couple who owned race horses.

He got to see me in action at first hand a few times, although thankfully keeping his pen in his pocket.

One particular problem with some drunken yobs started to get so much out of hand that Jeff told me straight: "Don, I want them out!"

There were about 10 of them altogether and they took a bit of shifting, but we managed to force them out of the door. There were the usual threats about them bringing in someone to give me a good revenge beating and this time I was in no mood to wait for them.

I knew these men worked in Glasshouse Street so the next lunchtime I paid them a visit in my XJS.

The staff recognised me as soon as I went through the door and the place immediately went eerily quiet.

"So you are going to come back for me tonight, are you?" I said. "If you do, I'm going to lamp you. You're barred!"

This was a case of taking the bull by the horns and it worked because they never came back. It happened at a time when there was a lot of bad publicity in the papers about door personnel, reports that led indirectly at least to the council deciding to issue its own badging scheme. I'd like to think that this reporter saw the job being done the right way.

Naturally I used plenty of threats, but the heavy stuff was kept to a minimum and our door was protected for the sake of our real customers. That in essence is the way to do it.

I even looked after the Odeon Cinema with Trevor for a while. Perhaps my main memory of that was after there had been reports of viewers ripping up seats during the Rocky film in the 80s. Needless to say we made sure the film, exciting and powerful though it was, was treated with more respect here.

Doormen were becoming more and more in demand. The situation was that if the police got called out five times to a particular establishment, they'd get a personal call from the licensing authorities and be told in no uncertain terms that they needed to have security.

This would obviously be something of a mixed blessing as far as they were concerned. The presence of doormen meant then – and still means now – that trouble was expected there. And, more importantly as far as the owners were concerned, it added to their wage bill.

Such places would employ minimum staff and, as soon as the immediate threats had died down, get rid of us again. I've really got very little respect for such folk. Money rather than security is clearly their priority and I simply can't work like that.

If I was called in to a place, I'd research it thoroughly and tell the management what the security needs were. Experience would tell me just how many men I'd need and where and I'd then tell the management my findings.

Unless they were prepared to do the job properly, I usually wasn't interested. And that would normally include a contract to assure me that they would be as good as their word.

There were plenty of venues close by in the busy city centre and the camaraderie between bouncers of a few years ago was clear for all to see.

If we saw that another pub or hotel was short on a particular night, we might lend them a man or two and vice versa. Also there were some very interesting sights sometimes when doormen would converge on trouble makers from different directions.

One memorable night I came out of a city centre night spot and literally stumbled across a drunken brawl. The scene was one of complete mayhem with about 50 or 60 people fighting toe to toe and doormen from the varied pubs and clubs in the area right in the middle of them.

I played my part, dropping one guy, and my mate Mick put a couple more out of their misery, but that was one incident where we were very grateful for the swift attentions of the police. Again it made very interesting reading in the local evening paper.

There was a sense that the doormen were all working for the same cause.

It was the same generally with getting into clubs for social occasions. Being a respected doorman tended to push me to the head of the queue, one perk at least of the job.

A typical evening would end with us popping in to McCluskys for a pint or two at the end of a night. There'd be a whole host of doormen there chatting about the night's experiences. We all felt like we were part of an important team.

I must admit that the gangster side of being a doorman has always appealed to me. Dressed in black and ready for anything, I've never been too far away from the action. It might shock some people but I have a genuine and abiding regard for the Kray brothers.

Whilst the violence, at times, got out of hand, there were rules within rules among gangsters and everyone knew the score. The Krays meted out their form of justice, but people never took the mickey out of them. There was respect and awe, I suspect, amid the fear they evoked.

Obviously I can't condone the fact that Ronnie and Reggie were finally brought to book for the murders of George Cornell, Jack 'the hat' McVitie and Frank 'mad axeman' Mitchell and sentenced to life.

Yet their image was something I honestly aspired to. I've always felt that by remaining a man of few words, a man of mystery if you like, I generated respect, even awe, among my colleagues and the people I was paid to protect.

And, if I could get that image across that to mess with me would be far more dangerous than it was worth, I was halfway to doing my job.

For every incident that ended in fisticuffs, there were literally dozens that were aborted by a withering look or a timely word – and that is really what a doormen's role is all about.

Over the years we've also been called on to do a fair bit of private security work, again a result of word-of-mouth recommendations.

We got contacted by a mother worried about the welfare of her daughter who was due to give evidence in court against her former boyfriend. She had been going out with this lad, but packed him up because he had been violent towards her.

The police got involved and he was charged. Then she had the problem that he'd be present in court and he began phoning making various threats over what he was going to do to her if she took the witness stand.

We picked her up in the Range Rover and took her to the magistrates' court in Nottingham. Denis stayed with her throughout the entire hearing whilst I waited outside in the car in case I was needed. Apparently the lad took one look at Denis and when he realised he was her bodyguard wisely decided caution was the better side of valour.

Also, in a domestic context, we were approached by a lady in a park in Nottingam who had separated from her husband and was worried about what he might do to her when he came back to the house to collect his stuff.

We contacted the police and were waiting for him on the day he had threatened to come. On that night he never showed, but another more convenient day was arranged and this time the visit went off without any major incident.

Coming back from working at one of the traditional events in Ashbourne, Derbyshire, I was recommended by Michael Sladell, from The Royal Hotel, to help a company that had suspended some of its directors who had then made threats to get their revenge.

We had two security men on the job when the men arrived and there was no earthly way they were going to gain access into the building. They made a couple of futile attempts before giving up.

Settling debts is another familiar part of private security work and I've done a fair bit of it. It isn't something I particularly enjoy doing and there are some incidents that I wouldn't particularly wish to repeat here because they got a little too violent.

But when a friend sold his Mercedes estate car I did get involved on his behalf. This bloke paid with a combination of cash and a cheque that duly bounced.

When I paid him my first visit I was quite polite and suggested that he should either return the car or pay me the money.

I was told very bluntly to leave or his workmen would bury me on their land.

So back I went a couple of days later, accompanied by some of my security staff, and this time I was in no mood to return empty-handed.

I told him I was going to take the vehicle and he responded by saying he'd call the police. I then turned the tables on him by explaining how futile that would be in his position and made a few threats of my own.

In the end he offered me a cheque, but I obviously refused as I could not guarantee whether it would go through or not. So I left with the required cash in my hand and a torrent of death threats in my ears. But I never heard from him again.

I can still see myself doing more private security work during my remaining years. These days there is a particular need to combat stalkers as men become obsessed with females in a far from healthy way.

Later in this book, I outline my views on what I consider to have been the abysmal security surrounding the death of Princess Diana, but the killing of another lovely young woman better illustrates this point,

Like countless people throughout the country, I was completely gutted by the death of TV presenter Jill Dando, who was also a much-loved and respected lady.

No connection was established with her high-profile role presenting Crimewatch, but in my opinion that alone should have entitled her to a bodyguard and proper security. If that had been the case, I'm certain she would have been alive today as her bodyguard would have been alert to the danger the moment he discovered a strange man outside her house that day.

Instead the appalling Barry George was able to creep up on her unnoticed and extinguished a bright young life in an instant.

Incidents like that lead me to want to lend my support wherever possible to helping innocent people live their lives, which is what I've been doing through my work on the doors all along...

QUALITY HOTEL GEORGE, NOTTINGHAM
George Street, Nottingham, NG1 3BP
Telephone: 0115 9475641 Fax: 0115 9483292

5th December 1999

TO WHOM IT MAY CONCERN

Dear Sir

REFERENCE DON McCALMAN

I would like to confirm that Mr Don McCalman has held the agreement to supply our hotel with Registered Door Supervisors for over ten years at our hotel.

Having known Don since I took up my post as General Manager three years ago I have found him a very co-operative and professional sub-contractor, and recommended him to my colleagues in the hospitality industry.

If any further information is required please call me direct.

Yours Faithfully

Richard Parker
GENERAL MANAGER

Sun Valley Social Clubs

Sun Valley House, 161–167 Lower Parliament Street, Nottingham NG1 1DP
Telephone: (0115) 958 1202 Fax: (0115) 958 2926

5th December 1999

TO WHOM IT MAY CONCERN

REFERENCE DON McCALMAN SECURITY

We as a company have used McCalman security for the last 3 years and have always
found the Door Staff to be of an excellent calibre and are fully trained and hold the
relevant certificates required by the Local Authorities.

The service and courtesy given by Mr McCalman in the way in which he operates his
company is second to none.

Yours Faithfully

Peter Saville-Bradshaw
GENERAL MANAGER

As I wish to remember myself aged 21.

Proud dad with one-year-old Darryl in Lois Avenue.

My prize E-type Jaguar I bought when I was 37.

My Pride and Joy.

A family picnic with wife Jackie, her cousin Adrian, our son Darryl and Jackie's sister Natalie.

Jackie's dad Jack, with whom I got on increasingly well.

Darryl and dad.

Darryl with dad on his 18th birthday.

Winding down after a hectic night at The Royal.

Denis Thornhill, Dave Littleton and Terry, part of my team at The Royal.

The Royal Hotel.

Love of my Life.

Grandchildren.

My lovely Grandchild.

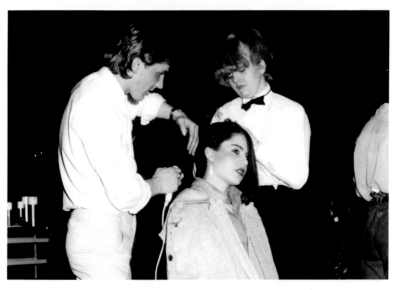

Daughter, Lisa gets a makeover.

Chapter 8

A New Era Dawns

CHANGE is inevitable in any industry. And the winds of change have been blowing through the private security field for several years. January 2005 marked the beginning of a distinct new era. For that was the date from which the Security Industry Authority's national badging scheme came into effect and no door supervisors are now allowed to work without their card.

Gone are the days of a door boss phoning up a mate, who was known to be a bit 'tasty', to get him out of a fix. We live in an age when everything not only has to be above board, but also has to be seen to be so. And, overall, I have to agree that it makes sense. It is just a crying shame, however, that at this particularly crucial time the experience of many a good door supervisor is being lost to the young people who face such an unenviable task in trying to step into well-trod shoes.

The call for legislation, it has to be said, was well made. Incidents such as the murder of Naresh Shah in March 2002 did much to influence public opinion. The 45-year-old accountant was stabbed to death one Saturday night in his own home by a gang of thugs, some of whom worked as doormen at a nearby pub. The doormen, who left their posts outside the pub for just nine minutes to carry out the attack, realised later that they had targeted the wrong house. Mr Shah had been the innocent victim of a gang of thugs who were neither licensed, nor trained. And, naturally enough, this incident was just the tip of the iceberg.

More locally doormen in Nottingham were the subject of a World In Action TV investigation during which it was clearly shown that some were actually dealing with drugs on the doors. I think that this, too, played a part in persuading the powers-that-be that strict action needed to be taken.

Going back to 2001, a total of 260 delegates met at the first-ever conference for bouncers. There they were told about sweeping legal reforms aimed at cleaning up the trade's image. Afterwards a police spokesman went on to outline that the Government had examined the industry after a series of incidents across the country where bouncers had been involved in drug dealing and other crimes.

He added: "I think doormen certainly have an image problem and I think this conference will go some way towards improving that." Would-be bouncers could, he went on, face tougher checks covering minor offences and any police intelligence held on them. Anyone with a conviction involving drugs or violence would be automatically excluded from working. All very laudable I'm sure you'd agree. Obviously something needed to be done to tackle the image of a black market culture that had spread from one end of the industry to the other, from the smallest 'bars' to the biggest security companies.

Talking the issues through with a friend of mine in the security business, Roger Adams, certainly throws some powerful points. Roger now works for his own company, Network Security UK, which is based at Mansfield. We got to know each other through working with Prosec Training.

Roger has trained door staff for 10 to 12 years during which time he has left his mark on doormen all over the country, including some who have subsequently come to work with me. We have also come into close contact through the ongoing development of the regulatory side of the industry.

Around seven years ago Nottingham City Council decided to launch a scheme gathering together figureheads from companies in order to provide mutual support. This is called the Door Watch Committee, of which I remain as vice chairman and Roger holds the post of secretary. Particularly during its first five years, the committee proved a very productive way for people to swap important information.

Once individuals got over their understandable inter-company rivalries, I think we all began to realise that we needed to work together in order to stay ahead of the game.

Like me, Roger mourns the fact that the new legislation effectively spells the end for a brand of doormen whom we were both very proud to have been a part of.

He says: "We've both been around long enough to have met real characters and been to venues of vary varied reputations.

> "Up to just a few years ago there were characters in every town and city working on the doors but, as with a lot of things, they are in much shorter supply now.
>
> "The doormen concerned – and Don was most definitely one of these – tended to be very well respected in their communities."

Roger pointed out that over the last 10 years there have been very substantial moves by local authorities and police forces, backed by peer pressure and influence from the Government, to clean up the trade. And this has already started to hit the characters that worked on the doors.

There have, however, as Roger goes on to say, been no such moves over the same period to clean up the customer base. Indeed far from it. Back in 2000 the number of new licences granted since 1995 across the country had risen by a staggering 38 per cent, building on a similarly disturbing increase in the period between 1992 and 1995.

Locally, in Nottingham the number of licences doubled in the space of just three years. Professor Dick Hobbs, of Durham University, who worked on a two-year study into our night life and security, highlighted part of the problem.

> "You can go back to since we've had taverns – there's always been someone charged with the task of turfing people out when they are unruly."
>
> "Today, security staff are really filling a vacuum left by the police."
>
> "We discovered in some cities you could have up to 30,000 people being policed by just a dozen officers, but there would be a couple of hundred bouncers there."

Professor Hobbs highlighted the market caused by club culture, which underwent a dramatic shift in the late 1980s.

> *"The patterns of drinking are different," he said. "It's chain drinking now, it's pub crawls. In the late 1980s going to clubs became cool again. Pubs started to imitate clubs in their decor in how they presented themselves."*

Bringing things a little closer to home, Nottingham's usual crazy Friday and Saturday night crowds are policed by around 20 officers.

Now don't get me wrong here... for I'm the first person to hold my hands up and pay my tributes to the police. In my opinion, and I've been closer to them in my line of work than most over the years, they do an absolutely fantastic job.

Let's face it, after the security staff have done their bit, it's the police who face the most unenviable task of all – that of controlling drunken yobs intent on throwing as much drink-induced rubbish at them as at all possible.

They have to make sense of very confusing situations and set in motion the powers of justice, often with very little support from the courts.

They have in my mind been totally let down by the Government by its controversial policy to allow the pubs, bars and clubs to open all hours if they so wish. You only had to look out on a Friday and Saturday evening to see what a mess we were already getting into before the legislation took effect. It is now routine to see a mass of drunken, mostly young, people swaying through the streets late at night, often with little or no regard to the traffic. Looked at from a sober perspective such a sight is both pathetic and worrying.

Often these people drink themselves into such a state that they barely know who they are, let along where they are going. It is all a symptom of a modern-day craze that is chipping away at so many people's lives – binge drinking.

The last few years have seen such a rapid increase in this phenomenon that it was little surprise that even this Government eventually chose to take notice. But what have they done? In my eyes, at least, they have potentially made a bad situation a whole lot worse. Yes, Tony Blair and his caring cabinet are so worried about what has been happening that they have allowed the prospect of 24-hour drinking.

Pardon my sense of irony, but I can scarcely believe their naivety. Talk about opening a jewellery shop to try to cure burglars.

Now, of course, I appreciate that for a host of practical reasons most pubs are unlikely to open 24 hours – at least not for now. But what they have done is open the door wide open, so that the pubs, bars and clubs can further take advantage.

What this means is that the licensing authorities, which from this point on are the councils, have very little power to prevent the tidal wave. In effect, licensees have been given a free reign to increase their opening hours as they themselves see fit, subject to possible scrutiny from a group of councillors.

Just think about it this way. A pub, with a sensible landlord currently in place, may get permission to serve from 7am, for example, so that sporting events from abroad can be viewed from the comfort of the local pub with alcohol on tap. But what happens when that landlord leaves? The place has then got the potential of being turned into an early morning drinking den.

Also has anyone considered the increased difficulties that the police are being caused by all this? Naturally, the mass wave of customers at both pub closing times and when the night clubs closed their doors later on was difficult enough. But I can't see that staggered opening times are any better. Not at all.

A significant rift has been brewing for some time now between the police and the Government on this particular subject and I know where my personal sympathies lie.

The Association of Chief Police officers spoke out against the law change in very strong terms. It said Chief Constables had "considerable concerns" about the move and believed, as I do, that it would lead to more binge drinking, more crime and more yobbishness. In addition Britain's top policeman Sir John Stevens urged the Government to delay its plans. The Metropolitan Police Commissioner warned that 24-hour opening would lead to more, rather than less, alcohol-fuelled trouble on the streets. Officers would, he said, inevitably have to be taken off their duties just to cope with the large numbers of drunks. He said: "The move needs to be slowed down. Large groups coming out at 3am or 4am will mean we have to man the streets to ensure they behave.

"There has been a deterioration anyway in behaviour." He added that "excessive drinking in extraordinary amounts" at weekends was one reason for the rising tide of attacks on our police.

There was a time, you see, when the police could safely predict what time the revellers would be dripping out onto our streets. Pubs closed at 11pm and the night clubs turned out at 2am or 3am. This meant that the police were able to organise their officers to meet the onslaught and that was it. By a certain time, major incidents apart, it would be job done. But how are they to cope if people are spilling out in their dribs and drabs completely out of their minds at all sorts of different hours, because that is the obvious result of deregulated hours?

Young people, who love nothing more than crawling in mass from pub to pub, will soon get to know that the next watering hole down the road is open for an extra hour, so the binge drinking will just get greater and greater.

The police's resources are over-stretched already and we're going to see our town and city centres more litter-laden and vandalised than ever before.

If that's not enough, listen to the words of Professor Robin Bloom, director of the highly-respected Centre for Social Research on Alcohol and Drugs at Stockholm University and regarded as one of the world's top experts on alcohol issues.

He said that, if the Government really wanted to tackle drunkenness and alcohol-fuelled violence, it should be seeking to restrict access to alcohol, with tight regulations on when it could be sold. Drink should also, he said, be made more expensive.

Professor Bloom warned that none of the measures in the Alcohol Harm Reduction Plan, published by Tony Blair's strategists, would help. "They are all there: school education, voluntary advertising codes, even a half-hearted discussion of alternative entertainment for youth.

"What it offers is a recipe for ineffectiveness." Instead, he added: "The historical control policies in England, including 11pm closing, have tended to keep problems with drinking relatively low by international standards.

"But that has been eroded over the years and now has been eroded still further by this step towards 24-hour drinking.

"Scientific literature from countries that have extended opening hours show that where hours are increased, the number of problems also rises. "A study of 24-hour drinking in Reykjavik in Iceland showed that the number of accidental injuries, injuries from violence and drink-drive arrests all increased."

Mr Blair's point of view was blasted, unsurprisingly enough, by Tory leader Michael Howard before his defeat in the May 2005 General Election. He accused the Government of recklessly encouraging "yob culture" and covering up evidence of the damage such moves have done in other countries.

More worryingly, in my view, doctors specialising in addiction have warned that the chance would fuel the spiralling problem of binge drinking and increase the toll of health problems related to alcohol.

Already in this country we are experiencing the self-destructive scenario in which casualty units on a Friday and Saturday evening are largely filled by people who have, in effect, been responsible for their own illness.

It fills me with anger to think that an ambulance may be delayed to someone who is having a heart attack for the sake of alcohol-fuelled youngsters who have shown no respect for anyone's health, let alone their own. Now don't get me wrong here. I have never in this book claimed to be a Holy Joe and I'm not starting now. I've been a drinker myself and got myself into a fair few alcohol-induced scrapes.

Until relatively recently, I used to go out with Denis and have my fill of booze to such an extent that I'd ask afterwards: "How did you get me home?" He'd reply: "You weren't that bad, boss!" and he was right, certainly compared with what you see in the streets of Nottingham these days I was as sober as a judge. My drinking largely had no adverse effect on anyone – except myself! When I came home from a busy night on the doors, I'd crack open the fridge and down four or five bottles of lager that gave me a thick head and took away much of my Sunday, then my one and only day of rest. But, at least, I wasn't harming my family or my employers.

Imagine if I'd drunk myself into peaceful oblivion after my shift, yet was expected to turn into work later that same morning.

New research has shown that more than half of UK employers feared that throwing open the pub doors longer would have a bad effect on productivity at work.

A survey released in August 2004 estimated that the total cost to UK business of alcohol abuse – combining the cost of drink-induced sick days with lost productivity caused by hangovers at work – at £2.8 billion per annum. The survey then quizzed 8,500 UK employers and found that 51 per cent believed the new system would cause a further drain on the work place. Perhaps even more worryingly almost a third of respondents suggested that it is now more acceptable to turn up to work with a hangover than three years ago. Being self-employed for the vast majority of my working life I have been away from the office environment for many years but, boy, they must have changed a lot since I did!

Martin Warnes, the manager of Reed.co.uk, said: "It is interesting to recall that the licensing laws were first introduced because munitions workers in the First World War couldn't perform their tasks properly.

"Perhaps the Government should have borne this in mind before trying to introduce a European drinking culture through legal changes."

Personally, I can see people going into work sizzled out of their heads and more driving their cars whilst still under the influence.

In the past many folk have sensibly safeguarded their licences by not taking their cars to the pub, but have had no inhibitions about getting behind the wheel the next morning. They thought, quite wrongly in many cases, that their bodies would have absorbed any alcohol they'd drunk the night before and there'd be no problem if they were stopped by the police. Certainly if you're out until 3am or 4am on the juice, there's no way you can get into your car safely and drive to the office.

Naturally there are still sensible folk around who know when to stop. They are the ones who aren't going to so easily get seduced into drinking for longer and longer just because the opportunity is now there. But, as we all know when we've had one or two already, the temptation to stay for just one more and maybe another after that gets greater and greater. Peer pressure is a strong influence as we don't want to go home because our friends are still drinking.

So, before we've had time to think things through, we have reached the next stage where we've drunk so much, we couldn't care less what happens.

By that time, issues such as how much money we've got for drinking or what time we told the wife or girlfriend we were coming home have literally gone to the bottom of the pint pot. Of course, I'm being a bit naïve here because these days women are perhaps more likely to be a pint or two ahead of you in the pub rather than waiting at home with a cold dinner! There's no doubt in my mind that we're going to see more and more people getting themselves into debt and family life, which is already under the greatest possible strain in this country, suffer even more. The longer opening hours inevitably mean a greater demand still for doormen, yet we are beginning to get into real problems here.

Many people work the doors to supplement their regular income and the prospect of doing longer and longer hours may be very impractical for them. So I can see less and less of a security presence to meet a greater and greater security threat.

We shouldn't be too surprised at such apparent madness from the authorities. After all, they are merely following their god of this awful age – money. Councils and the Government want to screw as much money out of us as at all possible and beefing up the lucrative night-time economy still further understandably appeals to them.

Our Prime Minister insists instead that longer hours won't mean more drunken violence. Instead law-abiding citizens will just be able to get a drink at their convenience.

Flexible pub hours will result in a "more relaxed attitude towards drinking", they say, instead of the culture where people slam down as many drinks as possible in the crucial final minutes before closing time.

All this would make sense if the Britain of today was a more continental-style café bar society. But the problem is that we are not.

We'd all love, in theory, to see the city of Nottingham frequented by families sipping coffee and sharing life experiences into the early hours, but we also know it is just never going to happen. The climate is not conducive to such a utopian environment for one thing and our drinking culture has been moving in entirely the opposite direction, under the express guidance of the greedy authorities, for far too long. You only have to mention Britain and booze abroad and you know where we stand. Holiday resorts throughout Europe have to make special provision for the Brits whom they know are going to get pissed out of their heads and turn their peaceful havens upside down. You only have to look at the mayhem caused by supporters of England and the various leading club football sides to appreciate that the link between excessive drinking and violence is all too well established.

The Daily Mail highlighted Nottingham's plight in a topical feature on the city's nightlife in January 2005, showing that it is not just because of gun crime that our ever-worsening reputation is spreading far beyond the borders of Robin Hood county.

Admittedly, drugs and the crazy pace of modern-day life are significant factors in the malaise, but there can be no doubt that alcohol is well at the top of the list of explanations for why we are becoming almost accustomed to anarchic behaviour.

You can imagine that is particularly gut wrenching for a person such as me who has given so much of his time to regulate our nightlife to see this tragedy now unfolding in front of my eyes, but feel totally unable to do anything about it.

My point, as Professor Hobbs hints, is that doormen are out of necessity more and more in demand these days even apart from the ever-escalating number of licences.

Today there are an estimated 100,000 doormen in Britain, but it's the nature and quality of this modern breed of security staff rather than their numbers that we need to take a closer look at. The Government has taken the industry forward by insisting on badges and the nature of training for our doormen of the foreseeable future. Today instead of being trained purely on the job, you have to go through a course and become a qualified door supervisor in six months.

If you can get past the police checks and get on with the training course, you should be able to earn yourself a badge and a secure future, if you pardon the pun, on the doors. It all boils down to a 30-hour course done over just six nights or two weekends.

Topics covered by the training include a review of both licensing and criminal law, first aid, emergency management, drug awareness, health and safety, evacuation and emergency procedures. There is a test paper including all of these areas.

The second module then takes a look at conflict management and observing human behaviour. Candidates literally watch videos and answer questions on what they observe on the film.

The way that we, as door supervisors, can deal with incidents now has been regulated and this is much for the better.

Naturally in my time I have seen plenty of staff lose their heads, usually in very aggravating circumstances. We've all heard of stories of doormen throwing people down stairs or going in so heavily with their fists that guests get injured. And I'm well placed to know that it has happened frequently enough to cause alarm in the past.

I would, however, urge head doormen of the future not be naive enough to think that they are getting the final article when someone completes the course. Usually I would have a new doorman working directly with me for a few weeks to get an idea of his character. In particular, I need to see how he copes when the pressure is really on.

If he has the character qualities to keep his head and use reasonable force, he is well on the way to becoming a valued member of staff. But, if he loses his temper and mixes it blow for blow, he needs to be dismissed on the spot – and that's just what I've done.

The point is that you have always needed iron-like discipline to be a good doorman but all the more so in today's crazy world. But, in my experience, you can't guarantee this just by going through a course. You'll only really know a person's capabilities when they have been put to a real test.

Roger Adams's views on the type of doormen we are breeding today make for sobering contemplation. Remember he is a top professional trainer himself.

"I would say that a good 20 per cent of the core group currently learning to become doormen would have struggled in the past to gain employment of any kind." Roger feels, as I do, that modern doormen – and tomorrow's doormen unless we do something about it quickly – may well be less well equipped to do a much harder job than our generation. And that is worrying.

"Don't get me wrong," he says. "You don't necessarily have to be an 18-stone beef cake in order to be a professional doorman."

"But looking back on people who have been successful in the industry they have needed both to be street-wise and also physically capable."

For, despite the Government's own form of makeover for the industry, image remains of paramount importance. Today's drunken yob, like the yob of yesteryear, will size up door staff and decide whether they are going to take them on.

Put crudely, if you look a bit tasty and obviously take care or yourself, you are more likely to be an effective deterrent than someone who is 5'2" tall and 10 stones dripping wet. It's a matter of common sense. The problem is that the job appeals to young people – understandably enough – for its glamour value and the chance, quite bluntly, for men to pull a few birds. Yet it is more dangerous than it has ever been before, particularly as so many of the experienced men have decided to call it a day.

Being brutally honest, I can hardly say I blame them. To maintain the chance to do the same job that so many have done with such distinction for so many years, they were being required to be re-trained and pay out £300 for the privilege of gaining their badge. And, let's remember the badge needs to be renewed every three years. Now £300 may not seem like big bucks to top executives, but it's serious cash to honest-to-goodness folk who have worked the doors for as little as £30 or £40 a shift.

I'm no professor of mathematics but by my rough reckoning that means they have to work between eight and ten shifts just to break even. Ask yourself, how many people in other industries would be prepared to do that? Personally, I did decide to renew my own badge. So, at the grand old age of 64, I can still work the doors for another three years when called upon. But nevertheless I agree with Roger that had I been just a plain doorman and not a supervisor with his heart and soul firmly in the industry, we, too, may well have taken this opportunity to call it a day and I know that many people have taken this view.

I think the legislation would have been more effective had the authorities insisted that teams of door staff have at least one person who has a reasonable number of years of experience. Then there would be more chance of newcomers getting the right guidance because, as with almost all jobs, 90 per cent of your learning comes from actually doing the job. So what is the future for nightlife in the city of Nottingham where currently about 500 doormen ply their trade on a typical weekend night? Well, a quick look at the city during these evenings – and I can promise you that I prefer to view it from a distance, if I possibly can – reveals a worrying picture now that unrealistic attempts to change our drinking patterns have collapsed and drugs are so much more of an every day issue.

Today's Nottingham includes four or five distinct areas which all warrant priority attention. The Waterfront, Slab Square, Parliament Street and the Lace Market are heavily populated by lively bars and need to be planned for.

Resources can get sorely stretched when new venues are developed and require still more doormen. It all adds up to a picture when we are matching maximum demand with minimum experience and I worry about the consequences.

No one is arguing that we should go back to the old days and there's no doubt that badging and training are good and necessary innovations.

Yet, if we are not careful, we will lose the benefits by presenting today's recruits with a job they will soon find is not worth the so-called glamour and attention.

Chapter 9

True Lust and True Love

FOR MEN, there are few subjects, if any, as complex as women and sex. I can only guess that the creator is having a good laugh at our expense because knowing the fairer gender is a learning curve that drives you around the bend and, by the time you've started to gain knowledge from your mistakes, it's all-too-often too late.

Call me slow off the mark, if you wish, but I now appreciate that there is a huge difference between the two oft-misquoted 'L' words in the title to this chapter. But, boy, has it been a long and painful journey. There were times, mostly between my two marriages that I revelled in the hunt for sex with as many women as possible. That, without doubt, was motivated primarily by lust. Yet, today, when my looks have all but gone and I am no longer the centre of attention in a crowded room, I've discovered more about the inner beauty and personality of women, albeit more in theory than in practice.

Lust, it has to be said, was the main reason my first wife Sandra and I got together. Fairly unaccustomed as I was to the delights of the flesh, I took to physical intimacy like a child with a new toy. I simply didn't want to put her down. Intoxicated by the fact that we couldn't keep our hands off each other, I think we got married with a view to plenty more of the same. If only life worked out as easily as that!

Never wanting to waste a minute, I used to come home at lunchtime and whisk her off upstairs for a good, healthy lovemaking session. But such intense attraction, however magical it might seem at the time, inevitably fades, more often in months than in years. Then the question that couples face is over what is left. In our case, when you pricked the surface of our relationship, you found the answer, sadly, was 'not a lot'.

Faced with such a harsh reality, you can see why sometimes I reflect that, if it weren't for women having various bits and pieces, most men wouldn't have much to do with them at all. We'd probably live on Mars and Venus blissfully ignorant of each other save for a good pair of breasts! You're getting a picture of my first marriage by now. So perhaps you'd not be too surprised that, far from mourning her departure past a few pints and a raging headache, I saw the split as a great chance to further my sexual adventure.

Now, instead of having one gorgeous sex object in my lair, there was the promise of many, many more. Nottingham had a reputation of being a young man's paradise with notably more women than men up for grabs and I took my fair share. My aim was not to find the woman of my dreams for life-long love and commitment, merely to persuade the next person I fancied to share my bed. There was no shortage of takers. Those were the days of the real Don McCalman, physically at least. Blessed with jet-black hair and a good physique, I had enough confidence in my appearance to realise I was a head turner. All that was left, then, was to take full advantage. If only I could take those looks and combine them with the experience I have gained today. Then I'm sure I would not now be living such a lonely life.

The attraction between a man and a woman is both natural and wonderful. Realising that there is that precious chemistry between you is a feeling that takes some beating. But it doesn't necessarily mean that you've found real love. As the young woman, who so closely nursed my wounds after I'd been involved in a fight to save my mate Brian Barnaby, said, once a man has got what he wants, in this case, sex, there's no guarantee he'll come running back for all the extras that go with it. I think I saw her another twice!

One-night stands, I've had a few, but then again too many to mention. There were times when I didn't have to wait until the next morning and a hangover to wonder how I'd got myself into such a mess – I'd sometimes have gladly packed up and gone the moment we'd finished having sex! A few ladies, however, muddied the waters by uttering those immortal words: "I love you!" I didn't mind reciprocating in the heat of passion, but that was as far as it usually went, I'm afraid. Sorry, but when it's a question of lust or love, the odds are at least ten-to-one on the former! That's just the way life is when you're young.

I've experienced most things in my close encounters with women, including what is many a red-blooded man's distant fantasy – sex with two babes at the same time! A woman I knew and fancied often said she'd like the shirt off my back – it was a sexual compliment I enjoyed. One evening we met up for a drink at a hotel in Nottingham Road and it appeared that three might be a crowd. She turned up with a friend from up north. The consolation for the apparent inconvenience was that she, too, happened to be drop-dead gorgeous. We had a fair few drinks and all got on well. Then it was back to my friend's flat in Sherwood. I was naturally hoping that the evening would somehow have a happy ending for both of us.

Suddenly she shocked me by saying: "I can't sleep with you tonight, Don, unless you sleep with my friend, as well!" Now that was a sacrifice I hadn't anticipated, but was all-too-eager to make! The next few hours were a chemical haze. I made love to both of them several times over. It's surprising what seeing another beautiful naked body waiting in front of you does for your recovery time.

Eventually I gathered my stuff together – my thoughts would follow a bit later! – and got a taxi home. I went straight to bed at about 7am and didn't re-join the waking world until about 8pm at night. Let's just say I was completely physically knackered and ached in parts you can usually just dream of.

Meeting women was equally easy at work as it was at play. There was more than one occasion when plumbing wasn't so much a job, more an experience. I remember going round to one lady's house to sort out her heater. But, obviously, she had something a little hotter on her mind as she followed me into the bathroom and gave me an energetic snog. That was the start of a brief fling as I found that I needed to visit a few times more just to ensure that heater was still working! She told me she'd just got pregnant, but was having problems with her boyfriend. Those were two very good points in her favour – the first meaning I had little to lose, the second giving me a clear pitch.

That was until I knocked on her door one day and discovered that the absent boyfriend was actually very much in residence. Strangely enough I never felt the call to check on her heater again!

I was equally at home in the pubs and clubs. On one occasion a lady waltzed up to me in a Nottingham pub and opened up with: "You've got lovely brown eyes!" Within a few minutes, she was checking out the rest of me too.

Others were a little subtler. I was taken off my guard when an attractive blonde came up to me in a nightclub and said: "I'm sure I saw you on the train today!" Now I knew for sure I hadn't been anywhere near a railway station for months, but this was no time to look a gift horse in the mouth.

I'm afraid she was a bit off-track there because if I'd seen her I wouldn't have had too much problem remembering her. I could scarcely have forgotten. We got talking and it turned out her dad owned an engineering company and she wasn't short of a few bob. Not that it would have mattered to me if she hadn't had two pennies to rub together. I was soon smitten. She gave me her phone number and we arranged to go out for a meal in Nottingham.

This was one of those occasions when two people clicked. There was plenty of physical chemistry between us and when she was breathing down my neck as we went home in the car my mind, at least, was quickly turning to between the sheets. But this was one time when it just didn't happen. I'd drunk quite a lot of champagne during the evening and the ensuing heartburn wasn't going to do too much for my lovemaking, if you see what I mean.

I did see her again and she must have meant something to me because I was very straight with her. I told her there and then that I was otherwise engaged and, once again, was very surprised by her reaction. "All right, I understand," she said. "You may be seeing someone else, but there's definitely something between us and I'd like to go out with you again."

For whatever reason, however, it never really took off from there. I think I knew in my heart of hearts that this could have got serious, but that it was neither the time, nor the place.

There was a period when I fell out with a few mates because I had a reputation for temporarily taking their girlfriends off them. Mind you, one of my friends wasn't complaining too much after I'd taken one very attractive young lady out for the night. We went for a drink down the pub and ended up, as I'd planned, at her flat in Sherwood Rise. We had sex and I got my taxi back home and, as far as I was concerned, that was probably the end of the matter. Later I got a phone call from a shocked mate who said the woman had been so keen to get my phone number off him that she'd offered him sex as well! I understand that he went back for the sex, but never did divulge that all-important number. That's loyalty for you!

I had no particular dream image of a woman. They could be blonde or dark haired, tall or short, but they did need to have a curvy, feminine figure. Call me what you like but skinny girls have never really been on my map.

One of the most beautiful women I ever came across was actually during the early days of my marriage to Jackie. I'm not proud to admit that I failed on this occasion to keep my wedding vows but I'm trying here to explain what actually happened rather than what should have.

There are dangers that if you flirt with the opposite sex you could just fall in love. And that all but happened to me with a gorgeous-looking Italian woman, whom I met when my children were just three or four years old.

It all started when I was doing a plumbing job in Colwick. I just couldn't take my eyes off this woman, who was a couple of years or so younger than me. I said to the lads: "I'm going to go out with her!" So we arranged it. A friend and I agreed to take the woman and her sister, whom he'd secretly got his eyes on, to a pub called The Bendigo at Sneinton.

My mate pulled up in his van – he really knew how to turn on the style! – and we had a fantastic time drinking and laughing. There was no doubt in my mind where this was all going to lead. We went back to the woman's house – I slept with her upstairs whilst my friend entertained her sister downstairs.

Everything was wonderful, just as good as I'd imagined it to be. Until, that is, we were rudely interrupted by that very inconvenient thing called the next morning.

"You do realise that your wife will probably have the police out looking for us both," said my friend, with a worried expression on his face. He had a point that was exactly what I would have expected her to do. I decided I needed a reliable alibi – and quickly!

I rang a friendly businessman in Beeston and he agreed to the story that we'd been up all night playing cards. Those games of whist can get a bit heated at times! Altogether I went out with the Italian woman for about six months but, gradually, I think Jackie began to suspect something was amiss.

Certainly there was no way the woman realised that she was going out with a married man. I used the old excuse of working late to pick her up and take her to a pub at Burton Joyce. It could very easily have got very serious. The woman had never been married, but had a daughter aged about seven or eight from a previous relationship. And she was certainly not short of a few quid. She was forever buying me things, which took a bit of explaining away when Jackie spotted two leather coats and some perfume. And, being a typical Italian, she was a tremendous cook and took very little persuading to try out her skills on me.

I was in many ways a sucker for such a liaison, as I'd never really got women out of my system. I'd married far too young at 18 and, in all probability, far too quickly again at 21. Perhaps if I'd done the normal lads' thing and had a string of flings in my teens and twenties and got wed a bit later I wouldn't have been so vulnerable.

Then one day my luck ran out in unexpected fashion. I opened the door and to my complete shock there was the woman's sister. She had come round as part of her work, not expecting to see me and certainly not Jackie and the children. I thought that would be the end, but I was wrong. "My sister says you're married!" my girlfriend said the next day when I saw her again. But, instead of kicking me into touch, she made it quite clear how much she liked me and wanted to continue seeing me.

I went out for a couple more secret dates and this time she asked me to leave Jackie and go and live with her. It wasn't the easiest of decisions and I still sometimes wonder whether I would have had a good woman in my life if I'd decided the other way. But, deep down,

I loved Jackie more than I loved her and the children were an additional reason to persuade me to stay at home

Naturally my liberal lifestyle has got me into a few too many scrapes but, fortunately, I've had my fists to get me out of trouble if I've needed them. I was having a secret fling with one woman with a flash boyfriend with an American car, who was sending out people all over the place to try to track her down. One night I was in a pub in Carlton Road when she pushed a piece of paper in my hand suggesting the time and place of our next liaison. We went to a couple of clubs where a mate told me that this guy had found out about me and was going to send some lads down from London to straighten me out.

So I took the initiative and went round to this man's house in Nottingham. As soon as he opened the door, I hit him hard and true and he fell backwards into the hallway. I told him: "If you ever say someone is coming for me again, I'll bury you." In the end I was happy enough to hand the woman back to her boyfriend. She was trouble, which is quite a compliment coming from me.

Jackie, without doubt, was the love of my life. I've detailed elsewhere how I was captivated by her from the moment I set eyes upon her in a Nottingham street. Love is, of course, one of life's greatest mysteries and no one is quite prepared for when and where it is going to strike. It can and does often start in a very similar sexually charged way as the 'unreal thing', but soon develops in a much deeper, meaningful fashion.

Jackie was a very naturally attractive woman, who presented herself in a very appealing way. She was invariably well dressed – sexy, without being tarty, if you know what I mean. She was bubbly, easy to talk to and endearingly feminine. A true lady in every sense, she was the one person who was able to tame my natural excesses and guide me instead into the more peaceful waters of domestic bliss for the first and only time of my life.

I recall such happy days with her and our children. We'd go out into the countryside at weekends for a walk and a coffee, then call in to a shop for an ice cream and back home for a healthy salad. Even the small things in life take on extra significance when your eyes are coloured by being in love.

Jackie was extremely house proud. She was clean and hygienic and looked after our young son and daughter so very naturally and well. She loved our Hillside house, as I did, but was far more content to be at home than I was. I'd be the one who wanted to take her out for a glass of champagne and a slap-up meal to make the most of our developing and comfortable lifestyle whilst she realised that she had steak on a plate, symbolically speaking at least, at home base.

Jackie was much more cautious when it came to spending our cash. She realised I think that moving up in our standard of living was going to my head and, in retrospect, she was right. She'd have put some cash aside for a rainy day, I'd make hay while the sun shone.

She was a big part of my working life too. We were partners in business as she took on largely administrative rolls to complement all the other things going on in her life. She also used to come out with me on many of my antique calls. We'd drive out into the Derbyshire hills, I'd take a close look at a chest of drawers and Jackie frequently would check out the jewellery

Like many women, Jackie seemed to be a natural multi-tasker. She revelled in running a family whether she was working with me or holding down a job of her own.

It never crossed my mind during the happy times that I would be anything but by her side. Issues of forming future relationships and the still more distant thought of loneliness were not even on my mental back burner.

Nevertheless there were the seeds of our eventual destruction in my erratic lifestyle. There were inevitably a few bust-ups, notably when Jackie started to suspect something was awry during my affair with the Italian woman. I was totally shocked when I came home one day and discovered she'd gone. She didn't tell me where but left a note saying that I needed to decide exactly what, or more precisely, whom I wanted. In fact my decision had already been made and I was just desperate to get her back.

I did my detective work and discovered she was at a cousin's house. So a couple of days later I was on the doorstep. I said simply: "I've come to take my wife home." We had a tearful and emotional reunion and I think she realised I was genuinely remorseful. It took nearly losing her to realise that love was too important to gamble against lust ever again.

One evening when Jackie was truly on the ball came when a friend called Alan and I wanted to go out for a few drinks. I knew it wouldn't go down too well with my wife. who was pregnant at the time, so I told her that I had a few calls to make and would be back later. But as I was driving down Carlton Hall, I got the shock of my life. A head popped up from behind the back seat – it was Jackie! She'd gone to the trouble of hiding in the car, so she could check out at first hand what I was up to. Good job it was no more than a drink we had on our proposed menu that night!

Another feisty encounter happened after we'd been out drinking and Jackie had been sick. I sneaked out again later on to a club and was busy talking to the manager when suddenly he told me my wife was upstairs in her dressing gown! She let me know in no uncertain terms what she thought about me going out when she was poorly.

Then she drove home at record speed in the Mazda with me in close pursuit. When we got home, she more or less thumped me. A taste of my own medicine, I hear you say. I suppose all this shows that there was a spark and hint of danger to our relationship – exciting when times were good, but admittedly tiresome to live with when things were less so.

A friend warned me when I went to prison that the very worst could happen to me. It's well known that the nick is the frequent home of Dear John letters as women take the chance to make the break when their men are behind bars. It was never as simple as that with us two, but at that time I never thought it would apply to me.

After disaster had struck and I lost both Jackie and our beloved home, I inadvertently saw woman in a much different light. They still looked beautiful and sexually appealing, but now they were something I needed protecting from, often at all costs.

Countless were the times I leaned on my fellow doormen to close ranks around me and tell women that I just wasn't interested. My heart was totally broken and it just wasn't within their powers to mend it for me, however hard they tried.

Today I look back on those missed opportunities with some regret. If only I'd been willing to open myself up to the possibility of loving again, maybe, just maybe, I'd be a different person today.

There have been relationships since, but nothing remotely as deep or long lasting. Naturally, I don't feel any guilt about women I have met since Jackie, I just wish there had been more. But it can be quite difficult to piece a new life together after the failure of an old one as I discovered when I started going out with a woman on my 50th birthday.

She had just ended a relationship and, in retrospect, I should have known better. She used to ring me at night and talk and talk. But, to be honest, she was very much still in a state of flux. When I had flu, a very rare illness for me, she looked after me and she actually became one of the relatively few people to be invited to my house. We used to enjoy going out for Chinese meals together and altogether 'went out' for about a year.

But eventually we decided the relationship just wasn't going anywhere and it would be best if we both went our separate ways. I think that even a year on she was still unsure of whether she had been better off quitting her previous relationship, so you could see that there was really nowhere we could go.

The other relationship was a few years ago and was with a woman I met from a pub. This time the boot was on the other foot. She was married, albeit unhappily so, and I was the single gent glad of as much action as I could get. And get it I did.

She used to come over to see me and we'd make love in the morning. Then we'd go out and have a nice walk and some lunch before returning to my place and often having sex again in the afternoon. I was getting what I wanted this time and would have carried on had fate not taken a hand. Sadly, for me, the woman got pregnant and I spent time persuading her that an abortion was the best option.

I took her to the clinic myself and paid for the operation. On the way home she held up a condom and said: "Maybe, we should use one of these in future!" But I shook my head. For me, it was a case of once bitten and her getting pregnant had really shaken me up. I basically ended the relationship there and then. She pleaded with me to reconsider but I was not for turning.

In the last few years I have 'fallen in love' countless times and in countless different situations, but it has always been in my mind. The sad truth is that in many ways my emotional life ended the moment Jackie walked through that door. It might seem fanciful to some to think that could be the case when it was so very long ago.

But time is not always a perfect healer, it seems.

I realise that I have constructed a formidable wall around me – no longer in the physical shape of the doormen, but in my own granite-like resolve to prevent myself from getting hurt. I promised myself over and over again that it could never happen and the result has been that no one has ever been allowed close enough to share my life.

I think of Jackie, as she was then, aged 39, and the other women I think about are invariably much younger. I just couldn't bear the thought of rattling along with an old woman. Yet I have to concede that I'm an old man myself. That's the unavoidable contradiction.

I look at women nowadays and realise they see me in a far different light. They're the ones with the looks and the sex appeal to demand attention from men. The boot is well and truly on the other foot. I'm still very much a man and think about sex and sexuality, but it is something I have to back off from too.

I've allowed myself to drift in my mind as though certain young women were going to fall for me. Women use much more personal language these days and, if you're a little off-track, it is easy to mistake a compliment for something more inviting.

I know I can be the perfect gentleman. I yearn not so much for sex itself but for company and that distinctive scent of a woman. I long for a hug, a sign of affection that goes beyond the occasional peck on the cheek.

Yet with each day and week that goes by the prospect of finding true love again seems more and more like a distant dream. Perhaps I have found out the real difference between the two 'Ls' is that love can only happen once.

Chapter 10

No Messing...!

SOMEONE famous was quoted as saying: "The meek shall inherit the earth." Sounds good, but will being meek get your car fixed in modern-day England? You see, the real Don McCalman is not just a doorman by night, but a doorman by nature. And it certainly affects the way I live all aspects of my life.

I admit to being very individual in the way I approach life – when my mate Dave Sankey refers to me as The Legend, he is drawing attention to the fact that no one in his or her right mind messes with Don. Arrogant and rude I may be and I've certainly made more than my fair share of enemies even away from the doors, but there is actually a method in my madness.

To understand me a little more, you need to appreciate that I do have high standards. I would never ask of someone anything I wouldn't be prepared to do myself, but I am more than willing to take people at their own word. If they say they are going to do something, I expect them to do it. Is there really too much wrong about that?

I have always been a very hard worker, both in my professional and domestic life, and I am a stickler for things being done right, whether it's on the doors on a Friday or Saturday night or the service you receive from a shop assistant. What I really take exception to is a person who faithfully promises you one thing in front of your face, then goes and does precisely the opposite when your back is turned.

We live in a society where people all-too-often go through the motions and appearance of doing the right thing, yet symbolically, at least, they're thumbing their nose at you. Put simply, if you are happy to accept people taking the piss out of you, that's fine. But treat Don

McCalman in that type of fashion and you'll have so much trouble coming your way you'll never forget me. Mess with Don and you'll be the one who ends up in a mess!

Whether someone owes me £10,000 or 50p, the principle, as I see it, is just the same. I expect folk to be straight with me, just as I guarantee to be straight with them. Naturally it is a little easier when you're not short of money, but I do believe in paying my dues and on time!

My friend and work colleague Denis Thornhill knows how I operate better than anyone. After all, he is one of the few people who have regular access to my house as he drops in to pick me up each morning. Now I have often said I'd trust Denis with my life and I know that he would never steal from me however much he admires the antiques in my lounge. To contrast with my image as a grumpy old taskmaster, Denis earns more than a reasonable living and has the benefit of a schedule that is anything but dull and predictable. I'm even soft enough to treat my right hand man to lunch each workday at The Packe Arms.

But there is one condition. I ask him to give me £3 in a jar at home before we set off and, believe me, I wait for the clinking of those pound coins before I'm satisfied. Being generous is one thing I don't mind, being taken for granted is quite another!

Anyway what did I say about me and my car? I've never taken kindly to being fobbed off. During my marriage to Jackie, I had a problem with my Ford Zephyr. So I took it to this garage where they had a reputation for doing virtually everything, even signwriting. They put a re-conditioned engine in the vehicle, I paid the bill and that should have been job done.

But only a few days later the engine was misfiring badly, so I gave them a ring and asked them what they were going to do about it. The cheeky chap on the other end of the phone said they wouldn't be doing anything and, when I asked for my money back, warned that if I went to see him, he'd introduce me to a couple of his heavy mates.

That was a challenge I wasn't going to duck. I took a baseball bat to even up the odds a bit (one against three wasn't a good bet even for me) and they were only too pleased to give me my money back!

I'm much the same all these years later with my pride and joy, my Bentley. When it needed some repair work after being broken into, things didn't quite go to plan. The repairs were fine, but I was left without a functioning car radio. Next time I went for some tyres at the dealership, the bill came to nearly £1,000. I didn't pay there and then and it didn't take them too long to chase me up. "But what about the car radio?" I snapped back. "That's nothing to do with this," the man answered. "All right, then, see what you think when I drive my car through your bloody car showroom!"

The threat wound them up sufficiently for them to check out who I was and we were soon on the same wavelength again with a working radio! If I'd meekly paid my tyre bill, I might still have no music to drown out Denis's voice!

Car rage comes in several different forms – but I specialise in most of them. A few years back I was driving through Nottingham when I spotted a sandwich van by the side of the road. Feeling a bit hungry, I pulled over only for this flash guy, approaching from the other side, to almost casually clip me with his bumper bar.

He looked about 35 years old and had a couple of posh-looking mates in the car. "Are you going to phone the police then?" the driver shouted. "No," I replied. "But I need an apology!" "You apologise to me," he snapped. "I'll count to ten..." By the time he'd reached four or five, the impromptu maths lesson was over and he was sprawled out for the count himself! I just went up to his car, and as he poked his head out of the window, I nutted him as clean as a whistle! Funny enough, his mates left in about half the time it takes to say 'sorry'.

You might think I'm well over the top, you might even call me a brute, but what you can't deny that my way gets results.

My Bentley does bring the green eyes out in some people. And I don't usually rub people's noses in it by getting out my special car for just any old journey. On the other hand, I make no apologise for having it because it is my reward for working very hard. Once I did happen to be in my Bentley when I popped in to a chemist in Nottingham to pick up an urgent prescription. There wasn't much parking outside and I fully realise that I was technically breaking the law when I left my vehicle at a bus stop. But for the sake of a couple of minutes...?

Needless to say what happened next. I was striding back to my car as the traffic warden was in the act of sticking a £30 ticket on my car. "Don't you dare stick that on my windscreen," I shouted. "You've made your point."

But Mr Jobsworth wasn't satisfied. "Is this your Bentley, sir?" he said. "You realise you shouldn't have parked here," preparing to pull out a second ticket! By this time I had a small audience of people gathered across the road waiting for my reply. "Ok, you've done your best," I said. "The £30 fine means absolutely nothing to me and I'm going to get into my Bentley and drive home. You've got your commission, so just get back on your bloody noddy bike!"

I could see the onlookers laughing, probably wishing they'd dare to speak up if presented with such an opportunity. You see, I've had my fill of traffic wardens and I find them a pain in the neck. If they were genuinely concerned about keeping important roads clear and ensuring public safety that would be fair enough. But, in my view, they are usually just chasing money. On that occasion the bloke was being deliberately patronising because I drove an expensive car, so he needed slapping down. In any case the nearest legitimate parking space was nearly half a mile down the road.

Usually, however, I take a much more reasonable approach when confronted with officials of the law. This is the result partly of my great respect for the police and partly because I have learnt you get on better that way. So, if I get stopped by a policeman, I will merely say something on the lines of: "Good afternoon, officer, I realise I was in the wrong there. I apologise."

It is the reverse situation to when I'm the doorman and I am waiting to see what kind of attitude I get from a customer who, I've decided, isn't coming into The Royal. If they are polite and understanding, I'll guarantee they'll be admitted next time, but if they come out with a volley of abuse and threats they might as well never come back because they're not coming in! The police have a hard enough job already and if they're given a mouthful of cheek they're likely to come down on you like a tonne of bricks.

But if I'm dealing with salespeople, customer services staff or advertisement reps, well that's another matter altogether. In my view they're fair game for a really hard time and all of these types of people have had more than a few well-chosen words from my lips.

You simply can't go anywhere in these crazy times without receiving hassle from someone on the phone. I sometimes think my mobile should carry a Government health warning and that's nothing to do with supposed radiation. A few months ago I was wandering innocently enough round my local Asda supermarket at about 9pm when the phone went.

I couldn't believe it, but it was so and so from a finance company I'd never even heard of having a dig at me because I was a few pounds short on a payment from a credit card. Never mind the fact that I'd done business with the bank they were representing for a good few years and had a very reliable record.

Anyway I listened to his boring introduction and then cut in. "Just two things," I said. "Firstly, never ever call me at this time of night again and, secondly, just f--- off." "Do you realise this phone call is being recorded, Mr McCalman?" came the reply. "I don't care about your recording," I answered. "Just stick that tape right up your backside!"

It might not have been the most eloquent response, I readily admit, but it was probably what most of you would think in the same circumstances. I'm just bold enough to go ahead and say it because, quite honestly, I don't think I've got that much to lose. After being put in prison and losing your wife and home, there isn't much else anyone can do to you. I also just refuse to be intimidated by people for no good reason.

The other salespeople who often get a flea in their ear from me are advertising representatives. They have long since played a part in my life, as I've always believed that advertising is a worthwhile investment. But if they are going to chase me for advertisements, I think the least they can do is ensure they get my copy right and are prepared to sort things out if they do go wrong.

In my experience, however, the bigger the company, the more problems I have encountered. I've lost count of the difficulties I have had and am still experiencing with two major companies, although it is better on this occasion that I don't name names.

Let's just say that I have often enjoyed turning the tables on reps. They'll be on the phone giving their point of view when I'll say 'I'll be straight round to see you at your office and we'll see what you are going to do about it then!" It is really immaterial to me whether their office is in Nottingham, London, Glasgow or Belfast, I've been prepared to back up my words and go to see them face-to-face because that's just the type of person I am. On countless occasions the direct approach, however unorthodox, has produced the best results.

My friends say they enjoy hearing me on the phone because they know I'm very likely to give the other person some grief. I always give short shrift to anyone who phones me late at night, as I simply would never dream of doing the same thing in return. The same goes for time-wasters of which there are all too many. Mind you, I do pity some people when they leaf through the Yellow Pages for a plumber – they could easily get on the wrong side of me and then inadvertently phone another of my numbers and get a second helping!

When I buy something, I expect it to work. If it goes wrong and I'm under guarantee, I expect them to fix it. Follow my meaning? But life, it appears, is a little more complicated than that. When my new freezer was constantly going wrong last year, nobody seemed too interested in my complaints.

The company told me that I'd get a phone call the following evening and no phone call was forthcoming, so I decided to take the bull by the horns. I approached the shop where I'd got the freezer directly, yet they, too, seemed to be taking a casual attitude. The job it seemed would be done at their convenience. "OK, then," I said. "If I don't get someone from your shop round here tomorrow morning to fix my freezer, I'll take the freezer to you. I'll load it up in a van and get six bald doormen to dump it in the middle of your showroom. And they won't be going home without a new freezer!" You can imagine the scene, I'm sure, as various couples are innocently walking round the store when they are shocked by such an uncompromising sight. But, yes, I could and would have done it.

Needless to say, however, the repairs were carried out on time and there was no need for such a visit. I was able to chill out with a repaired freezer and the doormen had the day off.

But they are certainly useful folk to have on the end of a phone, you know. There was a time when I saw some blokes hanging around near my house and acting a little suspiciously. I went up to them and asked them straight out what they were doing. "Nothing to do with you!" was their gruff reply. Well, unfortunately for them, I happened to disagree. So I went round the corner tapped a few numbers on my phone and prepared to give them the shock of their lives. Just a few minutes later a van full of doormen pulled up and unceremoniously rocked their car on its way out of my road. As far as I know, they never returned.

Where money is concerned, it pays to be tough. After all, I run businesses, not charities and you need hard cash to look after your loved ones and put food on the table. When you get that gut feeling you're being strung along, you've got to do something about it.

This episode started innocently enough as I went to a bed and breakfast and installed two washbasins. I wasn't too concerned at the time when the woman said that she hadn't got enough money on her there and then. "Could you kindly come round and collect it tomorrow?" she asked. "I'll definitely have the cash on me."

Next day I called round as planned and the woman was nowhere to be seen. Her slightly anxious looking husband answered the door and explained: "Oh, she's out and she won't be back for quite a while. Actually she's gone to the bank. You can have the money by Saturday. "No," I answered. "It has got to be Friday at the latest."

Friday arrived but, surprise, surprise, there was no money. The bank she'd gone to a couple of days earlier must have been shut! So I decided on a very radical form of action. I picked up my hammer and in front of the woman's disbelieving eyes started blasting away at her new basins until they were reduced to a pile of rubble on the floor.

"Albert!" she shouted, attracting the attention of her husband. He came downstairs and I said: "Come for me and you're going to get it as well!" "You're never going to get your money now," the woman said. But I didn't lose out really. I knew full well that they weren't going to pay up, so I made sure that they couldn't get any enjoyment from property that wasn't really theirs. I must have lost £30 or so doing the work, but it was almost worth it!

Some time later I had a visit from an insurance man acting on behalf of the woman. "She says that you smashed up her wash basins!" he said. "Yes, I did," I replied. "But, actually, they were my wash basins." The shock on his face was a pleasure to behold and he simply couldn't get out of my house quickly enough. I never heard any more about the claim, but the insurance man probably dined out on that story for a good while afterwards.

On another occasion I quoted a bloke £6 and 10 shillings for putting in a new sink unit. When I'd finished the job, he came up to me and said: "Don't get me wrong, the job's good, but I don't think it is worth the money." I explained to him that I'd done the job speedily and well and, if I had charged by the hour, he could have ended up more out of pocket, but it fell on deaf ears. So, instead, I smashed the door of the sink unit. He threatened to call the police, but I wasn't bothered. Again as far as I was concerned I'd wrecked my own property.

There are times, however, when even the hard man has to smile. In our TV repairing days my mate Terry Bloomfield asked me to help him after he'd been threatened by this bloke who still owed him money. I decided to go round and pay a visit, but will never forget what happened.

The man went upstairs and, without even opening the window, hurled the TV out into the street with a gruff 'have your bloody TV set back then!' It landed in the middle of the road too close for comfort to a milk float. I couldn't believe my eyes.

"Are you going out next?" I asked. But, after that, I was almost lost for words because of the comic value of the incident. I merely picked up the pieces of what was left from the wreckage of a TV and took it back to Terry's shop in fits of laughter. It would not have been so funny, needless to say, if the TV had hit someone, but the whole incident seemed more like a scene from a film than mundane everyday life.

The same shop housed another horror sight when a man who, again, hadn't paid his dues, popped in for a chat. I weighed up the situation and, having calculated that we were unlikely to see any of the money, punched him across the room. His stunned body carried over a washing machine and landed with a thud on the floor. Fortunately he wasn't too badly hurt, but he certainly got the message.

I am fiercely protective of my family, particularly the females. Obviously much of what goes on is very personal and I wouldn't want to expose too much of the lives of people who mean so much to me. I am aware, however, that my daughter Lisa is wary of involving me with some problems because she knows full well that I'm likely to go in feet first. But I know she's also been grateful that I've lifted numerous weights off her shoulders.

For example, she was distraught when she had her car clamped and faced an £80 release fee. She told me about what had happened, so I got straight on the phone to the company concerned. "Do you know who I am?" I stormed. "My name is Don McCalman." The man on the other end recognised my name from the doors and within a few moments the £80 fee had been reduced to £20.

This is a subject that really winds me up and all I can say is that anyone who attempts to clamp one of my vehicles will be in for a battle. I've had one or two unwelcome warnings about my vans parked near my house but, if I ever found them clamped, I'd get the cutting equipment and sort out the job myself. They wouldn't get a penny and why should they? Too many of these people are just legalised robbers and I'm delighted that the Government has addressed the problem by ruling that wheel clampers must be licensed. In the past this business has just been a licence to print money at the public's expense.

I have also been very angry with some of the threatening messages left on my daughter's phone, usually without any justification at all. Such nonsense would not cause me any lost sleep, but it is a far different matter when it is directed to the elderly, for whom thinking they owe money is against their culture, and women.

Therefore I have no problem in phoning such people up and giving them a piece of my mind. Basically, if any of them contacts my daughter again, they'll find me on their doorsteps – and it would have to be a large debt to stomach that!

Dealing with such issues is more often than not a matter of how you speak to people. In other words the image you create. Take, for example, when I go debt collecting, a task that I do very sparingly indeed now, I might add.

My initial approach will be very reasonable. Whatever I have been told, I need to establish for myself that the money or property is indeed legally owed, otherwise I would be on very dodgy ground. But if it gets to the stage where I have to pay them a visit, I will cut a much more menacing air. They will see me pull up in a Bentley, wearing a black Cromby coat and black gloves. Immediately they open the door to me, they'll know that I mean business.

Then I'll address them firmly and carefully and let them know without doubt that I won't be leaving until they have sorted things out with me. It doesn't matter if they threaten to call the police – that would only expose their problems to a wider audience and you can't intimidate me like that.

The idea is to get the job done without anyone getting hurt or any damage being done. They'll get the idea that there's this crazy bloke at the door who isn't for turning and calculate it would be better for them if they co-operated with me.

On the other hand I wouldn't normally chase a debt owed by a woman, although I have been involved in a case for a close friend. The woman concerned would never need to worry about me, but I've been told that her boyfriend is a bit tasty. Against a professional, however, he wouldn't stand an earthly.

Say what you like, but being nice to folk just doesn't work – it takes putting a stick of gunpowder to their heads for many to get themselves into gear!

Chapter 11

Fairytale and Myths

SORRY, but I wasn't jumping up and down with joy when Prince Charles married his long-term mistress, Camilla Parker-Bowles, in April 2005. For, amid all the questions over what role this particular woman will or will not play in the future of our nation, my mind goes back to someone who made a real impression in my life.

I suspect that, like millions of others, we were not thinking at all about Camilla on that very muted occasion, but of the sparkling young life that was so tragically cut short in September 1997. It is difficult to say why the death of a young woman I'd never met, nor was probably ever likely to meet, was one of the most traumatic events of my life. But I would consider the untimely death of Princess Diana to be as sad and traumatic as virtually anything I've encountered, save for the death of my own dear mother.

You might think I'm crazy, or at least had a relapse from my usual hard man image, but every now and then I feel I see a glimpse of her in the sky. I'll be driving along somewhere, usually at night, and glance upwards, and there she'll be, a poignant reminder of a very special life. Besides the grief and churning emotions, I also feel a lot of anger for, as a professional security man myself, I will never be able to accept the official explanations of how she died on that fateful night in Paris.

When I think of Diana today, a very particular image flashes into my mind. Those memorable TV pictures of Diana playing with her then young sons, William and Harry, revealed so much about her unique appeal. For a privileged woman with the world at her feet she might have been, but she was also that highly approachable human being who somehow connected with our hearts. There she was in a relatively private moment showing the delight in her children – and the ability to communicate with them – that made us feel she really was just one of us. Before Diana came on the scene, I'd always had a respect for the Royal Family, a regard for their status and place in society. But, while she was with us, she managed to bring the Royals into our everyday lives in a way that can't simply be explained away by the million tabloid stories that were written about her.

I suspect I'm not alone when I say that I really wished I could have met her and her death was the end of a dream that could never come true. I recognised in Diana something that was also true of two of my other great idols, Elvis and Marilyn Monroe, and that was for a woman, who must have greeted literally thousands and thousands of souls, she had relatively few, if any, true friends. And, albeit in a rather more modest way, I can relate to her life. Diana lived in a palace, with endless riches and trappings, yet there remained about her a sense of loneliness. There was a very strong sense of a fairytale, not just from her whirlwind romance with Prince Charles when she first came to public attention, but in her whole persona. Even the thought of her supposed resting place on the island at Althorp House adds to that particular vision. I see her, rather like Elvis Presley, as lonesome, yet intensely loyal to those she regarded as her friends and able to reach out to the most unlikely of people. Here I am, falsely labelled by some as a millionaire, but living in a secluded house with locked gates and surrounded by antiques. I, too, have found that material riches and real riches are two very different things.

I feel the loneliness that she felt and a sense of knowing that I will always be misunderstood. The difference perhaps is that I built up my own shield, making it hard for people to get to know me and hard for me to know what they want me for. Diana, on the other hand, on account of her position in life was forced to live behind the Royal shield and tried everything she knew to break down barriers with the real world. She never knew, therefore, whether anyone she met was latching onto her fame, rather than relating to Diana, the human being. And the strange years that have followed her death have merely confirmed that many people, who told the world they were Diana's friends were in fact nothing of the sort.

You can't say you are a friend, then sell a story about that person to the highest bidder. And Diana has been a victim of such treachery more often than virtually anyone, both in life and in death. In my mind, I wished I could have had the chance to offer her the unconditional friendship she wanted. I'm convinced I would have picked up the phone and there she would have been, saying: "Don, you never would have guessed what happened today...." and talking as though we were on the same social level.

She did visit Nottingham, of course. The most notable occasion perhaps was when Prince Charles had broken his arm in a polo accident and she made the vigil to Queen's Medical Centre.

More personally, only a few months ago, through my antiques work, I came across a prime example of just why I consider the late Princess to be so very special. I got a telephone call from a woman wanting me to go and have a look at some prized photographs in her possession. She told me that she was the relative of a man who had contacted Diana after he had been involved in a serious car accident. Apparently the Princess had written back to him to say that she would visit him. He was amazed enough that she had taken the time from her hectic life to write him a letter, but never imagined he would actually get to meet her. Then one day she turned up on his doorstep in an XJS in their modest Nottinghamshire village. He could scarcely believe his eyes that a member of the Royal Family had come to visit him! Those photographs were treasured memories of a day that said so much about Diana's unique place in the hearts of the people of this country.

For, although privileged in her own life, she made the time not only to conduct important and well-publicised campaigns on important issues such as landmines and AIDS, but also to do things which no-one else would know about. I was so thrilled just to look at those photographs and imagine what her visit meant to an ordinary family from an extraordinary woman.

Naturally enough, I found her extremely attractive. She was a young and beautiful woman with a lovely figure, yet I could never relate to her in a sexual way. Obviously in the last few years there have been lots of stories about the alleged lovers that she took, and these have sought to diminish her reputation and give extra credence to Charles and his new bride, Camilla. But, as far as I'm concerned, such stories do not matter too much. She was a beautiful young woman and craved company in the same way that most of us do. I would like to think that she found love and companionship in her later years to in some way make up for the traumatic life she had with Charles. But I sense that there were always tears alongside the short spells of happiness. She was, to me, an untouchable, more a spiritual rather than a physical presence. And that comes from a man who, as you know by now, is truly red-blooded!

What she needed to know in those very vulnerable years after the collapse of her marriage to Prince Charles was that there was someone she could truly lean on – yes, a rock, and I don't even think that Paul Burrell fulfilled that role. Instead she was craved for her position in life, her great fame and her body. The stories of how Diana stood aside from the traditional restraints of royalty and offered her compassion to AIDS sufferers, victims of war and just mortal souls in need of a hug are both countless and well documented elsewhere. She made the Royal Family accessible to the hearts of the general public for the first time in history and somehow I doubt there'll ever be another like her. Yet such an unusual person was bound to make enemies and nothing will convince me that didn't play a role in her demise.

Most of us no doubt will remember where we were that fateful day in September 1997, when Diana died. But I was more shocked than most to get the awful news from my sister over the phone. I'd had the usual hectic Saturday night at The Royal and arrived home in the early hours of the following morning, having been kept well up-to-date through the radio and TV of what had been happening in France.

We were told that Diana had been in a serious crash, but that she was alive, if nothing else. But then I'm convinced that if everything had been done by the book, by the security staff and the medical authorities, then she would have survived. If it took a good while to accept that shock news, it took much, much longer for the meaning of it to really sink in. That next week was one of the most emotional in our history and my life, too. Amazingly, virtually the whole nation was in mourning. I lost count of the number of people who were surprised by the depths of their own reactions. For some reason, none of us felt really able to get on with our lives until after the funeral at the very least. We were left in the same state of emotional limbo that occurs when we lose someone from our own family. And the funeral itself was another memorable time. Practically the whole nation was glued to the TV that day.

I did some shopping at Marks and Spencer before coming home and watching. I recall listening to the words of Diana's brother, Earl Spencer, and realising that, yes, she had been so badly let down by the institution she joined when she first touched our hearts. And then there was the unforgettable version of Candle in the Wind sung by Elton John, which was so very fitting and conjured up memories of the death in equally mysterious circumstances of Marilyn Munroe. I felt so sorry for her lads and that sorrow has only turned more to anger in the years that have followed. For how do Prince William and Prince Harry feel now to be harassed by the paparazzi, knowing that they played a part in their mother's despair? They followed her wherever she went, even when she went to the gym to work out. And, of course, they were there doing their all too intrusive job on the day she died.

But let's forget about all the emotion for a while and just consider the facts. For me, they point to the conclusion that, despite the various investigations, or perhaps whitewashes, we have had into her most public of deaths, the real questions have remained unanswered. One of the reasons I feel so strongly is that even the very basics of personal security were not observed. We all know that Diana had been stripped of her title of HRH and therefore did not automatically get the type of security that would have been her right as a member of the Royal Family. But, even having said that, I simply can't believe the mistakes that were allegedly made by those who were supposed to be looking after Diana and her lover Dodi Al Fayed that night. I'm convinced that if these basics had been in place, Diana would have still been with us.

The first thing I would have said to Diana and Dodi is exactly what I told everyone I was paid to protect: "Just listen to me, do everything I tell you... and there'll be no problem. You're in our hands."

The head of security has extra responsibility for all his staff. Therefore not only does he not drink, but he ensures that even if there is the merest whiff of alcohol on any of the staff, they will be disciplined and taken off the job. Consider how much more important it is then that you know the condition of your driver. There is no way that the driver should be changed on the day of the job, for obviously you can't vouch for the condition of that person. I would have wanted to have the driver in my sights the whole evening, if possible. Unless that had happened, I would have driven myself. Instead we were told that Henry Paul had been off duty that night and that, as he had been called back to the hotel at the last moment, he may have been drinking.

I'm sorry, but that raises questions that I'm not sure that Mohammed Al Fayed, Dodi's father, or any of his staff could have lived with for long. We were being asked to believe something that was so naive as to be absolutely unforgivable.

The next very basic safety necessity is to have a car both in front and behind the main car you are seeking to protect. This immediately takes away the potential harassment from the journalists on their motor bikes but, more importantly, limits the speed of the main car. Next, there is the issue of the seatbelt. The official story is that the bodyguard, Trevor Rhys-Jones, who was in the front of the car with Diana and Dodi, was belted in, whilst his world-famous celebrity guests were not. Quite simply, I would not have allowed the car to start without knowing that they were securely belted in. And the same applies to any security staff who know their own business.

The bodyguard's story raises even more questions. Surely you would have expected a flood of words to come from this man, who was closer than anyone to one of the most dramatic events in history? But, no, he has remained silent.

The whole sorry episode leaves me with very mixed feelings about Al-Fayed. He may have been speaking for many of us when he shouted "'murder" after the accident, but it was a pitiful cry from someone who should have done more to help his son and Diana in the first place. In his care were the son he loved and probably the most famous woman in the world.

As far as I'm concerned, Diana was too popular for her own good. She had upset too many people with her open-mindedness and her unorthodox approach to public life, and perhaps there was the fear of worse to come. After all, those famous words were still very much in our thoughts. She had said: "I have news that will shock the world." Endless people have tried to explain what she meant – perhaps she was pregnant, perhaps it was something to do with the Royal Family. In truth, we will never really know.

But the prospect of her marrying Dodi, a devout Muslim, was perhaps the final straw. Everything from the ridiculously inadequate security arrangements to the unrealistically long time it took to get her to hospital and the endless inquiries that have followed point to one thing in my opinion: Diana was killed. Her light was taken out of our world because those people with different agendas wanted it done that way.

We'll never be able to prove it, of course, yet it remains for so many people a gut feeling – but one which, as a security professional myself, I know is supported by the facts. Maybe Diana really is in the sky looking down on our world. What she'd make of the fairytale Princess and the myths that have followed is really anyone's guess. It's fanciful, I know, but here's to the next world – may be then I'll meet her in person.

Chapter 12

Dustbin of the World

YOU can call me a true Brit. From day one I've lived in Nottingham and I have only been out of the country just once – and that was no further than Jersey. But does that mean I love the Britain of today? Do I hell!

You might suggest many of my thoughts are just symptomatic of getting old and you could even be right. I never thought that I'd be looking back and saying 'those were the days', but my problem with what is happening now runs a whole lot deeper than just nostalgia.

I know that a lot more people than would ever dare to say so will agree with what I am saying in this chapter. Surely as individuals we have a right to express our genuine thoughts without being unfairly labelled as racist? That freedom is something on which I thought our country was founded.

Yet there are many who are frightened to speak their minds for fear perhaps of losing their jobs or even worse. I'm perhaps in a better position than most. I'm coming towards the end of my working life and I don't even have to consider the effects my words would have on a spouse – in that way, at least, I'm happy to be a free agent.

I really don't mind what Tony Blair and the politically correct merchants who seem to rule our minds and our tongues think about me. I have been around a lot longer than our Prime Minister and have not been shielded from the real world like he has. He can live in his big house and his fairy-book world, but some of us have to deal with it as it really is.

The real reason that he would never confront the issues raised in this chapter are simple enough – he doesn't want to lose our votes.

Now you get an inkling why politicians are part of the dustbin we have created in Britain today. They are interested in power rather than truth.

I genuinely fear for the world – and in particular the Britain – in which I'll be leaving my children and grandchildren and I know all too many people feel exactly the same. I just happen to believe that major mistakes have been made in this country that have left England a less hospitable and certainly a more dangerous place to live.

I don't consider myself to be a racist and am not against immigration as such. Like many people, I have made friends with citizens of different races and recognise that some very lovely folk have found homes in this country.

If I saw an Asian man or woman being picked on in the street because of their colour and race, I'd be the first to intervene and help him or her, even if it meant going as far as putting my own life on the line. That's just the way I am.

My problem lies with the scale of what has gone on and what effect it may have on England in the very near future. You don't make yourself very popular if you say it, but Enoch Powell, the late and outspoken Conservative MP, wasn't too far off the mark with his famous Rivers of Blood speech in the 1960s. Mr Powell spoke of a time when racial tension would be a very dangerous part of life in Britain.

Well, just take a look for yourself at what is happening now. It is very possible that within 20 years white people will be in a minority in this country. I speak to many people and they tell me frankly that they will have left long before that happens and I can well understand them. If I was 10 or more years younger, I'd be looking for a future in a country that had more idea about what it is doing. It would surely not be difficult.

Political correctness has taken such a toll of our country that well intentioned folk are literally scared to speak out and express what they really think. Here in Nottingham, for example, it doesn't take a genius to realise that a lot of our problems are caused by tensions between gangs of different ethnic groups, yet even the police themselves are frightened to confront the truth for fear of being branded as racist.

After all, something very major must have happened to transform a city that was once such a pleasure in which to live into the gun crime capital it is known as throughout the country today. I would also contend that the massive increase in the availability of drugs and the significant rise of disease in this country is related, indirectly, at least, to the increase of immigration.

Yet at such a difficult time in our own country, all our futures have been made even more precarious by Tony Blair following George Bush's every move and taking part in the ridiculous war in Iraq. What the hell did he think he was doing?

It is now becoming accepted that the reasons this country went to war didn't stand up to the facts. Reports have emerged that there were no weapons of mass destruction in Iraq and there has been no evidence of a real link between Saddam Hussein and the terrible events of September 11 2001 when the Twin Towers were bombed in America.

The truth, of course, was that it was always going to be more to do with oil and power than morals. If these two key elements hadn't been involved neither Mr Bush nor Mr Blair would have been remotely interested. That's the way things work these days. So what have we actually achieved? Yes, we've got rid of Saddam, who probably wasn't much of a danger to us anyway, but now we have ignited street fighting in this dangerous part of the world. And, once hit-and-run street fighting starts, it very rarely ends quickly.

In the two years since the war officially ended we have been forced to watch on in despair as far more people have been killed than died in the conflict itself. Yet there has been no sign at all of Blair admitting he has made a terrible mistake – he's far too arrogant and stubborn for that.

The fact is that we've succeeded in involving ourselves in another Northern Ireland, a conflict that still hasn't gone away. For Bush and America, it all has shades of Vietnam. We are still committing troops abroad in a 'war against terrorism' that clearly can't ever be won.

It sickens me to speculate on the money we are spending on such an ill-considered mission when there are so many needy people in our own country. How about spending more hard cash on curing disease or helping our children? No, instead we have meddled with people's lives when we shouldn't have been involved whilst setting ourselves up back home as a time bomb.

It just makes me shudder when you think how many people have been allowed in this country with an agenda that would like to see the establishment here overthrown. In how many countries would this be allowed to happen?

You can come up with all the reassuring platitudes in the world, but there's no mistaking the fact that we now have folk over here who would gladly strap bombs to their backs and kill innocent people.

What kind of evil is that? Such scum are supposedly acting on behalf of their gods, whilst we just sit back and let it all happen because we're scared to say anything. Anger is merely going to grow and grow as the years go by and the result will be major conflicts on our streets. We have had a few grim tastes of it in the last few years in some of the cities of this country, but I don't think we've seen anything yet.

It's heartbreaking and of no consolation to me that I might be dead and gone before it really kicks off. My view is that the terrorists, as they are called, could hit us at any time. They will bide their time but, when they do strike, they'll strike hard. For they have behind them one of the most frightening exonerators of their outrageous behaviour – religion!

You don't need me to point out that, whether you're referring to Palestine, Jerusalem, Iraq or closer to home in Northern Ireland, religion seems to be a unifying factor in the problems we face when it is supposed to be the solution. I don't want to get into an argument about Islam, but it is a fact that we now have the awful prospect of fanatics killing themselves and others in the cause of their religious bigotry.

Not that I think the Church has much more to offer. I've only got one word for those folk who go to church each Sunday and try to wash their hands of what they have done in the week – hypocrites.

That sort of religion is no less manipulative than buying your teacher an apple to try and get on his or her side.

Is God so easily taken in? For all that is wrong with the Church, I still happen to believe in Him, but there's no way I need to go to a building every week to show other people.

England, as I know it, is disintegrating in front of my very eyes. We are fast becoming over-populated as we seemingly allow in more and more asylum seekers.

Once again I don't doubt that many have good reasons to flee the countries of their birth, but surely there has to be a limit? We can't keep increasing our population ad infinitum. To be honest even if there were to be stricter limits applied now, I truly believe that the horse has bolted. It's too late, in my view, to control immigration now, whoever is in Downing Street.

My work often takes me to Leicester, supposedly one of our great multi-cultural cities. But if you think that all is sweetness and light, you must talk to different people than I do. I've spoken with plenty there who are sick to the back teeth of it all and are just waiting for the chance to get out of the country. Who can blame them? I would definitely do the same thing if time was on my side.

All around me I see a country that's dominated by money and all other values are going out of the window. I've already made my case clear about Mr Blair, but I don't think any of the other parties have a realistic answer either.

They are all as bad as each other in my view and I just can't imagine either of the present leaders of the Conservatives or the Liberal Democrats ever making it to number ten.

Everywhere we are seeing the inevitable results of money being our modern day god. Let's consider what is happening back here in the streets of once-friendly Nottingham. The place has literally become over-run with bars over the last few years.

The police are virtually powerless to act as the nature of the place is changing so fast. At one time they knew what the difficult areas of the city were – as did the doormen – and they could make their plans accordingly. But now it could kick off almost anywhere at any time and there's no doubt what is mainly to blame.

You can talk about drugs all you want – and I do have my very grave concerns about them – but, for me, the most dangerous of the lot is alcohol.

I have been in one of the best positions possible to see how it alters people's behaviour. Now, don't get me wrong, I have always enjoyed a drink and, if it weren't for my health problems of today, I'd still be drowning my sorrows with the best of them. But today's binge drinking culture is frightening and very destructive.

When you've seen reasonable young lads turn into morons and, perhaps even more alarmingly, women turn into virtual prostitutes, you begin to grasp what I mean.

I think it is significant how the fairer gender has changed over the years. In my day the code of behaviour between a man and a woman was much different. You thought you'd really cracked it if you got a kiss and you might have to wait a good time for that. But these days you get the impression that young women would wonder what was wrong with a bloke who didn't try to have sexual intercourse with her after a night out. In effect, a kiss has become a shag.

Add the vast increase in the numbers of women binge drinking in recent years and you've got a very worrying social phenomenon on our hands.

It seems that, for some reason, young women are trying more and more to be like the lads these days And that can't be good news for either gender, in my opinion. There was a time when you could admire genuine femininity among the fairer gender, but that is becoming all too rare. Where it will all end? I really don't know, but perhaps this goes some way to explaining why the proportion of single people is on the increase.

Men might put a brave face on it, but, basically, we find it much harder to get to grips with the more fiercely independent and 'ladish' women that this culture is developing.

Certainly the family life of today leaves a lot to be desired. Here, at least, the eastern cultures seem to be well ahead of us in terms of people sticking together and supporting each other. Families worked best when the men went to work and women were happy to be at home and look after the house and the children.

I say happy, because I don't believe there were the same pressures as there are on women today to have a career. No doubt there are many, many people who just can't afford to live unless there are two reasonable incomes coming into the household. But, also, there are women who think they are missing out if they are not at work when may be they are actually missing out by not being at home.

Whether I'm right or not, I can confidently point to some people who are suffering – our children. We have developed a generation of latch-key kids, who don't know the meaning of a true loving home.

They fend for themselves most of the time and, on the occasions that their mum or dad is actually there, they are encouraged to watch TV or, worse still, play the interminable computer games that seem to be mind-numbing so many young people.

Maybe some day we'll wake up to what's happening, but, by that time, it will be too late.

In the meantime a visit to Nottingham on a Friday or Saturday night sees young people who scarcely know who they are and where they are, let alone what they are doing. I remember going into a hotel toilet and seeing a young girl completely naked. She was literally waiting whilst men just took their turns to have sexual intercourse with her.

It was horrible, degrading and potentially dangerous. In such circumstances you can only see sexual diseases increasing and increasing in this country and that's to say nothing of all the countless days lost to employers because of drink-related problems.

So, why if the evidence is so clear that something is very badly wrong, is little or nothing being done about it? The answer is obvious and it boils down to that one all-powerful force – money.

Licences are granted to people to run bars because it's a money-making enterprise – the social consequences don't come into it at all. As we look at society falling apart, ordinary people in this country are being hit harder and harder in their own pockets.

I can certainly understand people being up in arms these days about their over-sized Council Tax bills. First we had the Poll Tax, then the Community Charge and now the Council Tax. You can dress the bitter pill up in whatever different form you like, but it all adds up to much the same thing. Large amounts of money are going out of our pockets and for what exactly? Certainly the services we get seem to be under threat all the time and no longer match what we have to pay for them. I really worry for some people.

How can they be expected to fork out more and more money year after year? Does the Prime Minister increase pensions annually to ensure OAPs have the money to afford their bills? I don't think so. Everywhere we turn there are people all too willing and able to exploit us.

We might presume, for example, that the financial institutions would be on our side. Not a bit of it. Ordinary people are being plunged deeper and deeper into debt by unscrupulous lenders who are all too aware of our problems.

It is a well known tactic on their part to offer folk loans or credit cards pretty well knowing that they will be unable to pay them back. Then they subject us to verbal and written threats.

But, that's not the point – other people would be scared stiff by the mere mention of court action.

Contrast the lot of these often hard-working folk to loutish footballers who have got so much money they haven't a clue what to do with it. Their antics are an insult to people who have to watch their pennies so carefully.

To be honest, football isn't exactly my cup of tea and I am one of those Nottingham folk who does not mourn the fact that Forest are no longer in the Premiership. There's no doubt that the bigger followings of the nation's top clubs only brought more problems to the city over the years.

Mind you, even being a 'celebrity' is no insurance against being ill-treated in this country now. Given what happened to their mother, it is surely understandable that both Prince William and Prince Harry would be a little touchy where the paparazzi were concerned. Yet we hear of Harry being criticised for his strong reaction when lenses are poked into his face as he leaves a nightclub.

I tell you those parasites would have got a lot worse if it had been me. I'd have stuck their bloody cameras right down their throats. Then they'd have got some different pictures!

What can we say about the Government in this country? In my opinion they, too, are legalised robbers. Take VAT, for example – what is that all about? They just make up the rules to suit themselves and we, the ordinary people in this country, are the losers every time.

I've spoken elsewhere in this book about our justice system and needless to say I think our reputation for being one of the best in the world is ill deserved, or possibly just out of date. It makes my blood boil when you hear about one or two judges who have been prosecuted for child porn offences.

How on earth can they pontificate over others when they are living such lives? Again, when it comes to paedophiles, I can scarcely believe what is going on. You hear of cases of people being let out of prison when the criminals themselves have warned that they will probably go out and do the same things again.

Personally I don't think that we should be paying for them to be in prison at all. Abusing a child is one of the worst things anyone can possibly do and I can't work out why they should then have a right to live. Do you need volunteers to pull the rope? If so, I'd gladly do it.

Everything these days seems to be in favour of the criminals rather than the victims. You hear crazy stories from America of criminals suing those they have wronged and it's not that much better over here. We are told that we can use reasonable force to protect ourselves.

But what is reasonable force when you are worried that either your life or that of one or more of your family is at risk? The highest profile case, as I've already said, has been that of the farmer Tony Martin, who was sent to prison for shooting someone who was burgling his home. Naturally, I do have some sympathy with him, although I have to qualify it to some extent.

No doubt he was very frightened and I know that if anyone breaks into my house I'd be ready for him and not too worried about the consequences. I am well versed in the question of reasonable force, but I also go by the principle that if it's me or him – it's me who is going to live another day. If someone was coming for me, how do I know whether he has got a knife or a gun in his hand? As far as I'm concerned, a person loses his rights the moment he comes onto my property without my permission and I've got my shillelagh ready for just such an occurrence.

Once I did actually catch a bloke acting suspiciously on my property. He had come through the front gate and was peering in at the front window when I approached him from behind. I don't know what he saw in my living room, but I guarantee he was seeing a few stars after I smashed his head against the window. I have no sympathy for such people. One of the problems is that burglars know they are in for a good, long stretch when they enter a property in the first place. What have they got to lose by completing the job and either injuring or killing the occupants?

It's awful to have to think like that, but it's a cruel old world out there and getting more so by the day. I ask myself once again 'what would I have to lose?' After all, I've been to prison once and had my life taken away in a very real sense, so I don't fear protecting myself as I see fit.

God help anyone who threatens any of my family. Where the farmer went wrong was in continuing his actions when the attacker was seeking to get off his property. It's very much the same principle as with a doorman. He is well within his rights to restrain someone whilst that person is on the property he is seeking to protect. But, once they leave that property, they are the responsibility of the police and no one else.

Standards are also dropping in our shops and our businesses. As you might appreciate I'm a very busy man and can't afford to be held up too much during the day.

Anyway to avoid a potentially lengthy wait in Nottingham city centre I phoned up a store and asked if they could kindly put a pair of trousers out for me, so I could come straight into the store and get back to work as quickly as possible. When I arrived, I spoke to one of the staff and said: "Will you put them out for me?" And her answer was; "I don't know. Do you think I'm a clairvoyant?" Immediately I asked to see the manager and sorted it out. But you couldn't have imagined being greeted with such sarcasm even a few years ago.

On another occasion I gave £500 up front to an agent who has supposed to find me a place to live in neighbouring Leicestershire. A few weeks later I rang him and he told me he still hadn't found a place. He told me he'd keep me up-to-date but another fortnight went by and my phone never rang so eventually I lost patience. "If I don't get a cheque by Wednesday, I'll be on your doorstep!" He mumbled a few words about not having the money to pay me back immediately but, guess what, that money was there by Wednesday.

That's the way you have to be with people these days or there's always someone ready to take the piss. Nice people just get trampled on.

All in all I feel thoroughly justified in labelling my country the 'dustbin of the world' for that is exactly what it has become.

In some ways there's nothing I'd like more than to re-grow my jet black hair, roll back the years and become the real Don McCalman today. But that is no more realistic than Britain itself becoming the place that it once was.

No, in my opinion, England itself is no more. And that saddens me more than anything else.

Chapter 13

The Battle I Can't Win

JANUARY 1989 was, I believe, a fateful time in my life. For it was then that a death sentence was pronounced on me, although I had no idea it carried such an implication at the time.

Today most of us know enough to realise that diabetes is a very serious illness. About 1.8 million people in the United Kingdom are known to have it – that's about three in every 100. And, even more disturbingly, there are an estimated one million more who have diabetes, but are blissfully unaware of the fact.

Latest findings from the Department of Health suggest that within the next decade the number of sufferers will have grown by an alarming 54 per cent and eventually as many as one in ten of our youngsters will develop the condition.

The main reason, although this isn't something that applied in my case, is the rise in obesity in Britain. The bad news is that overweight people are more likely to become diabetics.

For a good 10 years I was in a very costly state of denial, I knew in my head that I had diabetes, but deeper down I hadn't really taken it in. But, unfortunately, ignoring something like diabetes doesn't make it go away, instead it merely gets worse and worse.

Like more than 75 per cent of sufferers, I have Type 2 diabetes. This used to be termed 'maturity onset' diabetes as it usually appears in middle-aged or elderly people, although it does occasionally hit younger folk. The main causes are that the body no longer responds normally to its own insulin and/or that the body does not produce enough. As a car driver, I liken my present condition to once owning an automatic, but now driving a manual. In short my pancreas no

164

longer does the job it used to accomplish, so I need more insulin to live.

Untreated, Type 2 diabetes can lead to heart disease, strokes, kidney failure, amputations and nerve disorders.

I'm not a man to make excuses, but my lifestyle has never been conducive to the discipline needed to manage my illness. Doctors have consistently told me that people with Type 2 diabetes need to eat a healthy diet that contains the right balance of foods. They will also make the point, clearly correctly, that too much stress is bad for diabetics.

As someone who runs his own business, my working schedule has always been hectic and chaotic. An average day might include a plumbing job, working on the drains, a cross-county dash to a sudden antiques call and answering a seemingly endless stream of enquiries about all subjects from the doors to advertising. I can't easily, you understand, be tied down in such circumstances to set meals and meal times. Throw in enough stress to faze a man half my age and you'll appreciate this is a cocktail for disaster.

I do, as I have stated elsewhere, make room and time in my hectic schedule for a lunchtime meal at The Packe Arms at Hoton, but otherwise I can hardly guarantee from one minute to another where I will be or what I will be doing. There is little time therefore to pro-actively check my blood sugar other than in the mornings and when I finally get home for the evening.

Ironically, my other handicap comes from the opposite end of the spectrum – the fact that in some ways I actually have too much time on my own. The temptation to give myself a treat and tuck into a delicious-looking cake or something equally naughty is magnified several times when I'm feeling bored at night in front of the television.

What does it matter if I bend the rules a little bit? After all, they say that a little that you fancy does you a world of good. Many a time I've convinced myself with such thoughts, but in my heart of hearts I realise that the harsh penalty is that I'm probably eating myself to death in the process. Just to give you one example, I should really limit myself to just a couple of biscuits, but all too often if I open a new packet I tend to eat the lot.

To be really good, I need to fill my diet with fish, salads, pasta, brown bread, low fat butter and the occasional steak, with just one alcoholic drink.

If I succumbed to the more natural temptation of say four pints of beer, a packet of crisps and a hot dog – as in a typical night down a pub – it would soon start building my sugar levels up.

All this is all the more awful and frustrating when I think that, diabetes apart, I have been and still am a very healthy man. You've probably heard of the type of person who has never had a day's illness in his or her life and hasn't darkened the corridor of a GP's surgery for years. Well that, until recently at least, was me.

I've pushed myself hard to stay fit and well. Having worked for myself since I was just 21, I've never given second best to a cold or even a bout of flu and taken a day or two off as you might do at a company's expense. Being the focal point of all my businesses, I've lived by the maxim that if I wasn't there, the job wouldn't get done. And being marooned in bed at home wouldn't pay the bills.

My doctors still tell me now that my heart is in very good condition and I've had more than my fair share of tests to prove it. All in all, I reckon I would be good for a further 15 years or so on the clock, if it wasn't for the diabetes.

The initial symptoms were bad enough, but I could live with them at least. I would pass water a little too often for comfort, undergo mood swings, have the occasional headache and feel plain irritable. I recall vividly being prescribed insulin for the first time, although I never appreciated then that, by now, it would be a matter of life and death.

It all seemed just a minor inconvenience back then. Injecting myself twice a day wasn't too much of a problem, in theory, although there were times when I didn't quite go by the book. But total that all up over a decade and it means that I injected myself around 7,000 times. And now that gruesome schedule has been increased to such an extent that I'm now injecting myself either six or seven times a day.

I wonder sometimes how I've got any veins left. I put my needles together in a sealed box and my bedroom drawers are literally bulging with them. There must be several carrier bags full and I go to the chemist every now and again so they can be disposed of.

One prick by a carelessly discarded needle and, as we all know by now, a disease as deadly as AIDS could very easily be passed on. But I can say hand on heart that will never happen the way I look after them.

Like everything else in my life, it seems, the diabetes has got considerably more of a hold since my 60th birthday. There are still good and bad days, but the proportion of bad ones has risen alarmingly, particularly in the last couple of years.

Generally the condition is at its easiest during the day, but the pain returns with a vampire-like vengeance during the evening. I frequently suffer from terrible pins and needles in my hands and legs – it literally feels as though someone is sticking needles into me. It is difficult to describe the pain accurately, but at times I can hardly bear to wear my trousers. Often my feet are so cold that I find it impossible to warm them up.

Recently the medics have sought to change my regime of drugs. They have told me that they will consider acupuncture because they are so worried about my mood swings. I've even been under the care of a psychiatrist.

I wake up with a fearful depression, so deep that I could often just pull the sheets back over my head and never surface all day. I'm saved, perhaps, by the fact that I have responsibilities such as getting Jason fed and watered and cleaning the living room as best I can before Denis arrives at about 9.30am.

I'm invariably more cheerful as lunchtime approaches and actively look forward to my only real break of the working day when I can sit down in the pub, sip a coffee and have a bite to eat. That's telephone calls permitting, of course.

But the pendulum will soon swing again back to the dark side. Denis says that I almost literally change character as I stride out into the car park ready to go back to work. He often refers to me as 666 and knows that it is at this critical time of day that he has most to fear from me.

Diabetes has helped to knock the fight out of me, particularly in the last year or so. Denis, to be fair, has tried his level best to help. He will always ask me whether I've got my insulin with me in the morning and will then ask me whether I have taken my tablets.

Altogether I'm on eight tablets a day in addition to taking my insulin. I often feel a bit like a guinea pig because different doctors and nurses you see regarding this condition often have conflicting opinions.

I'm sure that the cocktail of tablets is very counter productive. They are an attempt to combat my mood swings, but I think that they affect me in different ways.

It is well known that nearly all tablets have side effects and I think that sometimes my various forms of medication are actually working against rather than with each other.

You get a headache and the GP gives you a tablet for that and it gives you stomach ache and so it goes on.

I take one tablet that makes me feel more depressed, then to counteract that they give me anti depressants.

One moment I'm feeling fine, the next I'm completely down the tubes. My mood swings are literally that bad. And I'm convinced the drugs are contributing to that.

Altogether I don't feel like Don any more, instead I'm a tablets and insulin man.

My sister Pat was an SRN, a State Registered Nurse, and she is very sympathetic with my view that the drugs that should be my best friend are fast becoming my worst enemy.

I am beginning to think that my best option now is to go privately to get treatment that is faster and more effective. Certainly I've got to get things right sooner rather than later because time is no longer on my side.

I've had GPs phone me and say I needed to go to a clinic where I've been told that my toes could drop off. I have to guard against my feet going black due to poor circulation and be extra careful about any cuts.

I can be driving along in my car and suddenly feel as though someone is sticking needles in my ankles. The pain is so acute it literally makes me stagger. The worst of it lasts just for seconds, but it is surprising how long it seems when you are in pain.

At such times all sorts of thoughts run through my mind such as whether my daughter will find me dead in the middle of the night or what would happen to my dog Jason should I be taken ill.

It certainly makes me feel like ending it all. I'd like to think I'd have the guts to do it if I needed to.

I wander in my mind about living free somewhere, away from all my responsibilities, but diabetes is one of the things that holds me back. Say for example I went to Derbyshire walking for a few days and didn't have my insulin with me. If I didn't take insulin for several days it could be a matter of life and death.

Knowing this, means that I would really need to have someone with me, which in turn makes the idea a lot less practical. You can begin to appreciate the vicious circle.

Therefore I have the restriction of realising that I need to live within reach of quick medical care.

It is like living with a railing round me all the time, similar to being in prison.

I used to hear about diabetes on the radio. They gave the impression that it was none too serious as long as you looked after yourself. So I didn't really take in the significance of it all when I was diagnosed. I know now how serious diabetes really is.

I thought it was just a matter of sticking needles in me and didn't realise how painful that can actually be.

I inject myself in my legs and stomach and sometimes it can be very uncomfortable to say the least. Catch a small vein and it can make you bleed and there's also the worry of getting ulcers on your legs.

Diabetes can be a killer. If you get the flu or have a weak heart, you are more likely to die than an average person.

I had a real worry last Christmas when for the first time in my whole life I was laid up in bed for two or three days through the flu.

My blood pressure has always been fantastic, the level of a much younger man, I am constantly reminded, but I do have quite high cholesterol. I take garlic tables to try to counter that.

Because I have damaged nerve ends, I live with the fear that the diabetes could go on to attack my heart, my kidneys or even my eyes. It is possible to wake up blind in the middle of the night with this condition.

Sometimes I am passing water every hour in the night and that is caused by high sugar levels. My legs are then often sore.

I must have sweet things, but I know it is wrong.

My sugar levels have got to dangerously high levels on occasions and I know my daughter is worried about me. She now rings every day.

I find myself staring into space for ages and that's just not me. I have had this fear that something was going to happen to me for some time now with this edgy feeling each morning. In some ways it is actually far worse than the feeling of trepidation I had to deal with when I was in prison. I don't think I can live with this too much longer.

It is particularly bad to eat at night because then my system is unable to burn it off. This leads to high sugar levels and a restless night.

Also there's the worry that if I work too hard and don't take time to eat I can leave it too long. I am also worried that it may cause impotence. This, of course, is a very major concern to people in relationships and could cause matrimonial problems.

As for me, it's just another huge blow at a time when I've just about written myself off as being single for the rest of my life.

I've even been sent to a psychiatrist because of my continued denial of my condition. I've even started to stutter a little.

During the evening, I'm usually at my most lively and creative and am often full of ideas as I map out my schedule, as best I can, for the following day. If only I felt the same way the next morning when it comes to putting these well-intentioned plans into action.

My lifestyle has again come under scrutiny at clinics I've attended recently. They can't believe that a man of my age makes so many and varied demands upon himself and they'd be far happier if I calmed things down.

But it is a case, I'm afraid, of easier said than done. Sure, there is many a time when I'd like nothing more than to slip off and live quietly in the country, but I can't leave everything behind just yet. I have still got responsibilities both to the people I employ and also to myself to get a reasonable return for the investments I have made into my businesses through materials and advertising in particular. Also for obvious reasons I would need to temper my pursuit of freedom with the need to live fairly close to a hospital.

I've posed questions quite directly to nurses at Queen's Medical Centre. I've asked: "Will diabetes shorten my life?" and they have answered, quite honestly, that it very probably will. Even if they find a cure for diabetes now, it is all too late for me. The damage it has already caused to my nerve ends is incalculable and it can only get worse. My hope is to ward off the inevitable for as long as possible but, when I think about how the condition has deteriorated so rapidly in recent years, I fear I am fighting a losing battle.

I feel in many ways like a prisoner all over again. I can't even get out of my house and do a simple thing like enjoy a cold beer in a local pub. If I did, I know I'd soon be stricken by such an horrific pain in my side that no pint would be worth it. I have to be so careful what I eat and am bound by the discipline of insulin and drugs.

Am I being punished, I wonder, for my excessive lifestyle? Is God wreaking revenge on me for the pain I have caused other people in my life? These thoughts and more go through my tortured mind when the pain is at its most agonising.

I've been hit in every other way in my life including losing my freedom and my family, but health is the biggest loss of all. You don't appreciate it fully when you're fit and well, but without your health, it is much more difficult to work and enjoy any kind of quality of life.

If there's one lesson that can be learnt from my experience it is never to deny you have diabetes.

The quicker you accept that you've got the condition and develop a regime that accommodates it in your life, the better chance you have of keeping the worst of it at bay.

It might make you feel better at the time to shut off the reality of being diagnosed, but that feeling is strictly temporary. It's like downing a few pints to deny how you really feel. The truth is the longer you put off accepting the truth and adjusting your lifestyle accordingly, the more damage the condition will do to you in the meantime.

Here I am sitting alone in my chair every night wishing that I'd been that sensible. Instead my hopes of a happy and long retirement have gone out of the window.

If you take any message from this book, this would be a particularly good one...

Chapter 14

Sixty and Out

I'LL ALWAYS remember my 60th birthday. My friends and colleagues at The Royal did me proud by joining me for a fantastic party. It was a truly glittering occasion and it seemed that literally everyone came up to me that night and had a kind word with me.

About 70 were there in all, including my daughter Lisa, Chris Bailey, from the Door Watch Committee, doormen both from my company and others, and friends from Yellow Pages. Together we enjoyed a disco and buffet until about 3am. I organised the evening myself and it couldn't have gone any better.

It was a particular compliment to have Chris there as he has been a leading figure on Nottingham's doors for years. He told me that he'd be delighted if he looked as good as me when he got to my age and asked me what I'd like to drink. I appreciated the gesture.

The evening said so much about the camaraderie of people who daily put their lives on the line by serving on the doors. There exists a mutual respect that is rarely found elsewhere, I was really in my element. It was great to know I was appreciated by so many people and I still felt as though I had a role to play.

Yet even towards the end of the evening I had a sense of the emptiness that was to come. I began to drink more freely as though realising that this was the beginning of the end for me as I was getting too old to work on the doors. I'd both been looking forward to and dreading the party at the same time. I'd had a few notable bashes, particularly for my 50th birthday, but I didn't want this one to come along as I regarded my 60th as another nail in my coffin.

I found it very hard to accept my fast advancing years – and still do – and couldn't face the embarrassing possibility of people taking the piss and me being obliged to flatten them. Somehow it didn't seem appropriate.

I remember that I got home in the early hours and peeled off my black suit, my traditional dress for working on the doors, inspecting my badge with an unusual fondness. It was as though this was the last time I'd be wearing it.

For, as soon as all the excitement died down, a door was probably closing in my life that night. It was surprising how much of my life was wrapped up with my guests. Until then, I'd not only worked on the doors myself, but been seen around the city centre. Yet, almost from that day, I withdrew into myself and became what my daughter has occasionally described as a 'Howard Hughes-like character'.

Nearly 20 years of the same intoxicating Friday and Saturday night routine ended when I went home that morning. I had lived for that sense of anticipation and excitement as I carefully got myself ready at home, putting on the 'armour' that was so much a part of my image. I'd be thinking of what might happen, recalling some of the nights I'd already gone through and presuming that I'd live this way for ever.

Naturally, in more recent times, there had been the odd comment about my passing years. Occasionally someone would make a retort such as: "And what are you going to do about it, old man?", surveying my grey hair and beard. But I'd always been confident enough in my physical prowess to know that I could handle myself whatever went on.

I'd also enjoyed going out socially and chatting to all the doormen as I swept through the city centre. Everyone, it seemed, either knew me through personal contact or from my reputation and I thoroughly enjoyed it. But, since reaching the big 60, my way of life is so, so different. Apart from the occasional shift, my involvement on the doors is now limited to organising my fellow doormen.

I suppose it is rather like the difference between being a professional footballer and just looking on as a manager, coach or commentator from the sidelines. I still have many of the agonies from doormen going through their problems, the hassle of trying to fill a vacancy on

174

a door at the very last moment and the responsibility of knowing that ultimately it is my business, rather than theirs, that is at stake.

But I no longer have the buzz, the thrill of really being on the job.

Yes, I enjoy pulling up in my Bentley to pay the lads and being treated with much the same respect as when I stood beside them on the doors. There's still the familiar hush of "the boss is coming" as I get out of my car. And I maintain the same detached, professional image that has been mine all along. They'd say "hello boss" and I'd give just a half-nod or short acknowledgement. I still want them to know even now who is in charge and I would never allow them to get too close to me.

I pay them what is due and I pay them on time every week. I still don't think £40 or so is really enough for the trials that the men and women put themselves through these days, but that's the going rate. Then it's the drive home, but without the feeling of either a job well done or having pitted my wits against the worst that Nottingham's night culture could throw at me and coming out on top.

Socially, too, the attraction of going out into the city centre has disappeared. Even if I wanted to go out and visit a few old haunts, I'm dogged by the feeling that folk soon forget you and I don't want to subject myself to the full pain of that. Also, of course, I drink much more rarely these days because of my health which again makes it more likely that I'll just close my door for the evening, save for taking my faithful dog Jason out for a walk or perhaps doing some late shopping.

I've even grown my hedge to virtually overshadow the front of my house and protect myself from the world. I've always been a loner, but now I've become lonely. Very few people ever come to my house and as I swing open the door it is invariably my dog Jason who greets me. Bless him, he's the only one who is there for me all these nights.

What a contrast my current life is to the excesses of my youth and my married life, or even my experience of 10 years ago for that matter. For many years I was used to walking into a room and being the immediate centre of attention. Women would turn round and smile at me. I was very distinctive in my physical appearance, broadly built and confident with the ladies.

As I've said elsewhere in this book the women I've had have been remarkable and, to a large extent, I have few regrets. In fact you could say that, knowing what I do now and that my marriage was to end when I came out of prison, if anything I wish I'd taken more women up on their offers.

I miss the smell of perfume, the gentle touch, the chance to talk about other things rather than the rather male worlds of business and the doors. It would be nice on a day when simply everything seems to be going wrong to make a quick phone call home and say: "Love, we're going out tonight." We'd go for a quiet drink, a meal perhaps and talk over the events of the day.

It's amazing how things that seem so important at the time are reduced to mere trivia when shared with someone you love and care for.

My ideal lady would be attractive and articulate. I simply couldn't cope with an old woman and I certainly wouldn't want someone with nothing to say for themselves. It might seem hypocritical to some of you, but I could never wake up next to an old body and watch her patch herself up before going about the day. No, I'd much rather be on my own.

But the thought of having someone younger in body and in mind is what keeps me going. It would not just be sex, although that, of course, would be a wonderful bonus. There's so much comfort from lying in bed with your arms round someone and their arms around you. You feel warm, secure, protected. What could better that?

Yet I fear it is never going to happen. Even when I get the impression someone likes me, I instinctively put up my self defences. I know why it happens. I was hurt so badly when Jackie and I broke up that I simply could never allow it to occur again. I can't risk someone getting that close to me, yet at the same time, I need someone in my life, probably more desperately than ever before.

But how do you meet people when you never go anywhere socially? Nowadays when I'm in a pub people are no longer looking in my direction. I wish I could go back a few years and have the looks to go with the image of a successful businessman. To me a woman is a two-legged Bentley. Oh, how I wish I could have both.

But today when people look up and admire the view, they're staring at the car and not me. I've had the occasional woman say something like "I'd love to go for a ride in that", but I've backed off. I start thinking about what she really means and I conclude that she was probably just being friendly and wouldn't be interested enough to go out with me.

It's much the same with the odd compliments I get from the fairer sex these days. Some are genuinely pleasant towards me and, still being a red-blooded male, I can see how beautiful and attractive they are. Yet I feel as though I can't afford the rejection of giving it a try and being told they just wanted to be friends.

Although it is about five years now since I've had a real relationship, I still think in my mind of what it would be like to take an attractive woman to a restaurant, a stately home, or just for a walk. Would the other people be looking at me?

Perhaps, they'd be thinking 'what is she doing with an old man like him?' Then I turn round in my mind's eye and tell them: "Oi, do I know you? So what are you looking at then?" No, I don't think its weird or perverted for a man to go out with a woman 20 years his junior.

I used to gain comfort by going to one of my favourite places, Langar Hall, near Nottingham. There are few better things than having a sumptuous meal in the beautiful surroundings of a stately home. The service is superb, the food is simply out of this world and there's even the luxury of overnight accommodation. But the same sad scenario caught up with me. I was sitting having my evening meal when I heard a man on an adjoining table talking. All the rest of the room was full of couples and family groups and he actually said: "I really feel sorry for that man over there, sitting all on his own. Just imagine how bad that would be?"

I wasn't upset with him, but you can appreciate it was another dagger to the heart. Similarly the manager told me: "Why don't you bring a lady with you next time?" I didn't go back for a while.

Whilst this book was being compiled, I had the good fortune to meet a particularly attractive young woman, albeit as a friend. I did take her there a couple of times and the evenings were certainly a temporary boost to my flagging morale.

The woman concerned, Salena-Jo Marshall, who runs a beauty salon in Loughborough, showed absolutely no qualms about being out with someone 30 years older and even introduced me to her mum and dad. But I still had the feeling that other people must wonder what a woman like her was doing with an oldster like me.

I found it interesting that a woman like her – both exceptionally beautiful, business-like and intelligent – should be pleased enough to be in the company of someone far removed from her peers.

At least the experience is confirming my belief that there is some room in today's crazy society for a gentleman. For that is what I am to women now. I am a far different Don McCalman on the all-too-rare occasions I'm in the presence of the fairer sex. I treat women with the respect I feel they deserve.

I could never see myself living with a woman again. If you spend a lot of time on your own, which I inevitably have over the past 20 years, you get used to your own space and the way you do things. Occasionally, Jackie will come round and give me some help round the house. She may reorganise my jumbled office, or tidy up the kitchen. Naturally I'm really grateful for a helping hand, particularly as I am usually so busy, but I find it very hard if I can't immediately lay hands on something I previously knew where to find. I suppose it's a fear of losing control.

If I was with a woman, it would be short, but I couldn't promise it would be sweet! The very first time she greeted my appearance home with those immortal words: "Where have you been all this time?", I'd explode: "Probably the same place as you're going now!" and kick her out of the door. No messing. You see, you have to be a compromiser when you're in a relationship and all the more so if that relationship includes children. To be honest, I'm just too old and set in my own ways to bother with compromise any more.

I think the only being in the whole world who can put up with me 24 hours a day is my beloved dog Jason. Dogs are incredible creatures, far different from human beings in their sense of loyalty. Believe me,

I've been kicked in the emotional teeth time and time again and therefore find it very hard to trust.

Dogs are just the opposite. You can lose your temper with them, yet they'll come straight back wagging their tails wanting to love you.

Unlike humans, they appear totally non-judgmental. I get so annoyed with myself when I lose it with Jason. I might briefly take out some of my many frustrations of the day on him for no better reason than he is the only one here. I'll be busy tormenting myself with: "What did Jason do to deserve that?" but, as far as he is concerned, it seems to be almost instantly forgiven and forgotten.

I got Jason as a puppy and remember the joy of bringing him home. Then he'd got a long life ahead of him. Now the clock is even beginning to tick a little for him. He is seven years old and around halfway through his life. I know that I wouldn't ever want to be without him. At best, the day he dies I'll go completely off my head and whoever happens to get in the way will not know what's hit them. At worst, I ponder the thought of going with him.

Certainly if there was a choice between any of my fine antiques and my dog, it would be the easiest decision I've ever made. I'd sell the lot to extend his life even by one day. What is a vet's bill compared with all the love and company you get from man's best friend?

My typical week day starts at about 7am when I take Jason for a walk and vacuum and clean up as much as I can. There's no-one to take any of the pressure of running a home off me, although my daughter Lisa does help me with keeping my office running when she possibly can.

The phone lines will be already going ten to a dozen and I'm waiting for Denis to come round. We leave the house at 9.30am and it's time to get on the road. I will probably have antiques calls and plumbing and drain jobs already scheduled. We have two vans now and cover a very wide geographical area.

Basically, I'll go anywhere and everywhere for antiques provided I think it will be worth it and I cover the East Midlands as a plumber and for the drains. But no day will be without its additional complications. There are phone calls coming in all the time and I always have to be circumspect when I answer them.

After all, I don't know until they have spoken whether I'm wearing my antiques, fine arts, plumbing or security hats or, just maybe, they could be for Don, the human being. Those calls often alter the well-planned course of our day, taking us countless miles out to an urgent job just when we thought we'd sorted things out.

I do, however, insist on a lunchtime oasis. Denis and I almost invariably call in for lunch at The Packe Arms at Hoton. These days I have to be more careful about my diet because of my diabetes and I have to inject myself before every meal. But I enjoy the temporary relaxation of maybe a prawn cocktail or something else relatively light, washed down by two or three cups of coffee.

The staff like me in there and treat me with plenty of respect. To some I'm the man who sits in the corner, often on his own, often with Denis. Others know that I am a doorman, a bit of a man of mystery. Although there are still the telephone calls to disturb my peace, it gives me time to reflect. Sadly, I don't always like what I see. The mirror of my mind is probably even harsher than a real mirror, at least if I'm to believe what others say to me.

I've become an old man since my 60th birthday, but I just can't accept it. For some time I've had a strong feeling that I was approaching the final chapter of my life. I liken our time on earth to a pyramid and I'm on the way down. But it's not a soft descent, or a slow one in the manner in which we normally make progress in our lives. Instead it is harsh, sharp and potentially humiliating,

Time flashes by quicker and quicker. No sooner has one week ended but another has begun. No sooner has one year ended but we're seemingly on the verge of another winter, another lonely Christmas. Unbelievably, I'm no longer 60, I'm actually 64!

Among the few genuine joys left are my grandchildren. As I've stated elsewhere I kiss their photographs each and every day and think of them in my prayers at night. I love spending time with them and treasure every moment.

Those of you who are fortunate enough to have grandchildren will know what I mean when I say it is like having your children all over again. I think that, despite the sleepless nights and all the hassle, most people would agree that seeing your children in their first few years is one of the most wonderful things that this complicated life has to offer.

It would pay even the most cynical and hardened of folk sometimes to take off their cynical blinkers and tune in to their child-like view of the world. How lovely it is to suspend our usual disbelief.

One of them will chirp up: "Grandad, I'd really like to be like you when I grow up!" "Why's that then?" I'll reply, knowing exactly where all this is going.

"Aren't you a millionaire, grandad?"

"No, actually I'm someone who has worked very hard all his life, has some possessions and has saved a few pennies."

But, all the fun aside, I wouldn't like any of my grandchildren to imitate my life. Not at all. I hope that one day they'll appreciate that you should never judge a book by its cover and see how true that has been of my life. For what use are all the possessions in the world when you can't take any of them with you when you die?

If I had my time again, I'd do things a whole lot differently, particularly in my personal life.

I've cried buckets recently when I've seen their child-like drawings of me alongside their grandmother and they have asked me why that isn't the case. All I could do was to stall their question for it is so difficult to answer.

Recently the whole family got together for a Christening and the pain got to me again. For I knew that I should have been at the heart of the occasion rather than almost being on the outside. No matter how hard you try, the truth has a habit of kicking you in the teeth from time to time.

I honestly look at some of my closest friends, some of whom have not got half the things that I have, and I'm green with envy. They have been able to find companionship and lasting love in their lives and I haven't.

They can't understand me now when I tell them that I'm fast giving up on my dream of a woman to share my life with. But then they can't see inside me and appreciate the emotional damage that was caused all those years ago when I went to prison and then lost my marriage.

In many ways I've been unable to ever move on from that. It did lasting damage to my self-confidence and contributed hugely to the loner you see today.

Fortunately, I do get some comfort from my inkling that there really is more than all this.

The spiritual experiences I have described in this book in which I have seen my mum and dad after their physical death have added to my personal belief that we don't finish in the grave. This is one reason why I insist that I should not be cremated.

I think it is entirely possible that we come back to this world again and again and try to learn from the experiences we have already had. It seems logical enough anyway.

I've looked and seen death in the face, both in the form of my dear mum and dad and my friend Mick Alvey. It really is like looking at a shell. You see in front of you a body, the form a person special to you took in his or her existence, yet suddenly there's no evidence at all of life.

The brightness that once lit their eyes has gone and I'm convinced that the spirit has left the body, whether that be to return again or go to a more 'heavenly' existence.

Whichever is the case I earnestly believe that, as in the words of the haunting theme tune to Titanic, we do indeed 'go on'.

Don't worry, however, that the one-time hard man is going soft enough in the head to join those hypocrites who make their weekly journey to church each and every Sunday. They seem to think that by doing so they are getting in the good books of the one who created this world.

It doesn't apparently matter what sins they may have committed during the week just as long as they turn up in their regular spot and say sorry! And did I say that it was children who were naive?

Put in human terms, can you imagine a pupil giving their teacher an apple in the forlorn hope that they will become the class favourite. So, if ordinary human beings are able to see through manipulative behaviour, how much more must God know exactly what we're up to.

I'd prefer to think that God is much more straightforward than that.

When you are staring in the face of eternity, you realise that everything in this world is of limited value, even my beloved antiques. In a few years they will probably belong to someone else, perhaps someone who has never heard the name Don McCalman.

The fact is that you just don't appreciate life when you're young. It is as though you are in the fast lane of the motorway and everything happens so quickly that life is but a blur going on around you. Everything is just there and you just take it all for granted.

You worry about the most ridiculous things that either will never happen or, if they did, wouldn't matter a jot in the eternal scheme of things anyway. Youth is an indulgence, a party in which you attempt to gorge yourself while you can and presume consequences are something that happen to other people.

Oh to have a wise, experienced head to plant on young and broad shoulders. Instead in older age the spirit is willing and more knowledgeable, yet the body is comparatively weak, vulnerable and full of pain. That's one I'll have to ask the Almighty to explain if and when I get to meet him.

One consolation of my state of life now is that the man who always had to be number one in whatever he did suddenly has nothing to prove to anyone.

A Range Rover flashed past me the other day seemingly doing about 100mph. The old Don McCalman would have taken up the challenge and chased after him to show him who was boss. But with age comes maturity and an awareness that there really is nothing to prove any more. It would be the same with laying a lad on the deck in front of his mates and a team of admiring girls. What possible benefit would I get from that now?

I think that when I came out of prison I did have something to prove – to Jackie and to myself. I wanted to show her that I could still be a success, drive the fastest cars and live an exciting life, even if it was going to be without her. I literally 'bounced back' from my prison blues, ran a dozen successful businesses and enjoyed the trappings of what most people would regard as a good life.

But if I was to fall flat on my face now, there's no way I could scramble back to my feet. If I lost all my money, it would be for good.

If my health failed any further, I don't think I would still have the fight left to keep on battling against the odds.

There comes a time when you simply can't 'bounce back' and that's where I am now. I'd like Heartbreak Hotel by the immortal Elvis to be played at my funeral. The song reminds me so much of my relationship with The Royal and the story of my personal life.

For 20 years I have given my heart and soul to the place, yet it will always remind me of my break-up with Jackie. Just ponder the words for yourself and see what I mean. Yet very soon Jackie will have been with her current man for as long as she was with me. That hurts, even though I have a lot of time for him as a human being.

My sister, Pat, says that I am like a cat. I have had my share of nine lives already. Destiny took me along a certain route in life, whether it was with my full agreement or otherwise.

By splitting up with Jackie, my life went in a completely different direction. It took me back to the doors, back to business life and away from domestic security.

Through going down this road – although I would never have chosen it – I have influenced the lives of so many folk, some for good, others less so. Now I feel that I have literally been brought to a place of no return, a 'dead end'.

I can no longer taste any excitement to life and no longer have any reason to drive myself forward. It's too late to become a millionaire, too late to put back together my domestic life.

They say that, for some, life begins at 40. But, for me, my 60th birthday marked the beginning of a steep decline.

I regret not having the chance to take my mum and dad out in my Bentley. I wanted my mum, in particular, to know that the little child she lightheartedly chastised for getting into fights and scrapes so often blossomed into someone to be reckoned with. I'm convinced she would be well proud of the reputation I have gained over recent years.

Yet in doing so I've become trapped in a way of life that the medics and my relatives fear will eventually be the death of me. Whereas once I drank to drive away the hurtful memories, now I am working myself into an early grave.

Jackie says that by this stage my life should be simplified and with time for relaxation. And, of course, she's spot on. But the truth is that I've never listened to anyone.

One of the main reasons I've always been my own boss is that I hate authority. I just couldn't cope with the idea of being bossed by someone else. I wouldn't stomach it for five minutes.

But, more importantly, I've ignored the repeated warnings both of Jackie, my children and now my doctors. I've over-committed myself in my business life both in terms of finance and time and it is no easy thing just to walk away from it all, Like with my own mind, I've built my own prison and I just have to live with it. Everything seems to have lost its lustre in my life. The antiques that fascinated me so much have been reduced to mere objects. My work is now a matter of going through the motions and, socially, I feel as though I'm hardly living at all.

There are times, particularly at weekends, when I've barely got the motivation to get out of bed and, believe me, that's not Don McCalman. I've even started to let Denis work more on his own and told him straight that I'm fast losing interest.

I have a strong feeling that time is short and this book really is the last chapter of my eventful life.

I just hope that people reading it will not make the same mistakes as I have. Don't get obsessed by possessions and leave people behind. Don't think you always have to be number one in a crazy world and forget what is really important.

Sometimes even if you think you are right, it pays to listen to a second opinion.

All too soon, I'll be just a distant memory. It is surprising how quickly a human life is banished from people's consciousness. Who was Don McCalman anyway?

My answer is here in these pages. For this is my legacy to my loved ones, my friends, my colleagues and anyone else who cares to read it.

I've packed so much into my lifetime, far more than could ever have been recorded here, but I've also experienced the most enormous emotional pain.

They say that what goes around, comes around, and I honestly wonder whether God is having the last laugh on me.

Perhaps, because of all the trouble I have caused, He has destined me to come to a lonely, miserable end.

Who knows...?

Appendix

PREPARING this book has been a journey of self-discovery and much has happened both in my life and in the world during the year or so in which John and I have been working on it.

The first thing of which I am very proud is that I managed to gain the new door supervisor's badge from the SIA which means that, in theory at least, I'm fully qualified to man the doors until I am almost 67. Providing, of course, that I make it that long these will certainly be my last days both working on the doors and in charge of doormen.

As I have said in this book, putting aside regrets about my personal life, I have thoroughly enjoyed every minute of it and will give it up not because I want to but because there is nothing even I can do about the ravages of fast-advancing years.

Even if I wanted to, I don't think I could ever get away from the doors.

In the last few years I have deliberately not socialised in the city centre, where I was better known, but my past is always with me.

I suppose it may be something to do with the long black Cromby coat, the Bentley car and the fact that I more often than not appear aloof and alone.

It's my fault, of course, because I have carefully cultivated the image.

Wherever I go, people soon pick up on the fact that I am a doorman and I find myself either being asked to cover events or sort out this or that in people's lives.

It's a two-edged sword. On one hand I thoroughly enjoy what I do and, if you put a letter in front of me giving me permission to chase a debt, I have no fear at all. That's the sort of thing I'm good at and I'll get the job done.

In contrast, however, it would be nice to get away from all that. It's one thing to be admired and respected for what you do, quite another to be liked and wanted for what you are.

The people in my life all too often want a slice of me, but aren't necessarily willing or able to put anything back. I still feel as though I'm being pulled in all sorts of directions, but hardly anyone, apart from my relatives and a handful of friends, want to know the real Don.

I'd like to mention here my mate Dave Sankey, a fellow businessman and one of the most genuine friends I've ever had.

He rings me every day and is always there to offer a word of encouragement or advice.

A lovely family man, he's even said he'd be happy to find some land for me to live my countryside dream. He's that sort of bloke.

It is, in many ways, an anonymous world. We are all like ships in the night barely making contact with each other.

How I've managed to come through relatively unscathed is a mystery to me as well as probably to you.

Despite all the many threats and the fights I've been in – believe me, this book only details a few of them because any more might just be too repetitive – I've never been detained in hospital through working on the doors.

Yes, I've been a visitor to the casualty unit a fair few times and, several times when I've had a head injury, I've been advised it would be better to stay.

I've always declined because, quite honestly, I hate hospitals. They remind me of death and I feel that you must be very seriously ill to be in there.

Fortunately, I've only had to have one operation – for a hernia shortly after I came out of prison – and that's a real blessing because I absolutely hate the idea of losing control.

Even when they dig my grave, I'll insist they provide some steps in case I need to get back out again!

Yet I fear for the future of young folk taking on this daring and glamorous profession today in a way that was not applicable even in the hard sober days of my youth.

I do hope that in this journal I have not sapped you of too much hope for the future of Nottingham, Britain and the world in general. But I have told my story truthfully and realistically without any of the spin that seems to predominate so much of the media today.

We have major problems now dealing with both binge drinking and drugs that has propelled the level of violence in pubs and clubs to a new unpredictable level. And we are asking a new generation of door staff to keep the peace in a setting in which the breadth of the licensed trade has been determined not by need, nor demand in my view – but purely by profit.

It is a task that I personally would take on – because working on the doors is in my blood – but I could hardly heartily recommend to anyone but the very strong and able-minded.

Even whilst writing this, my fears both locally and nationally appear to have been confirmed. First we had what I believe to have been the heart-felt comments of the Nottinghamshire Chief Constable Steve Green that his force was "reeling" from dealing with 30 murders and excessive paperwork and was having to "borrow" officers.

He warned that he was so overstretched that he might, for the first time, have to "farm out" an entire murder case to an outside force.

The Tory leader Michael Howard followed up by citing Nottinghamshire as an example of where bureaucracy and paperwork were crippling the police and promised to scrap Whitehall's "target culture.

And shadow home secretary David Davis said Nottinghamshire was "an extreme case: of the problems facing police forces across the country.

"They simply can't stay on top of the crime. It's a spiral of decline," he said.

My home city has been labelled – justifiably in my view – as one of the gun capitals of the country. And the St Ann's Well Road area where I was raised is now a place where people live in fear going about their ordinary lives.

All of this saddens me to the core because Nottingham until recently used to have such a great reputation as a place in which to live and work, as well as a centre for night life.

Don't ask me for answers. I think I have already hinted where I feel we have gone wrong. Even more disturbingly, perhaps, we have all been shaken by the terrible London bombings and its aftermath.

I am not a racist, but I just wish that the powers-that-be had listened to that lone voice in the wilderness back in the 1960s.

Now we have had the first suicide bombers in this country it is hard to see a happy ending. Extremists of all denominations are a danger to us all and, as a country, we have only ourselves to blame.

The war in Iraq, as many observers have stated played its part, as did our indiscriminate immigration policy. Now we are adopting get-tough measures after the horse has surely bolted.

Maybe what I have written in this book will be taken more seriously as a result. I honestly believe that this once great country of ours could be on the verge of a civil conflict that will be the unholy legacy of political decisions that are already coming back to haunt us.

What I do know for sure is that, for all we lacked in terms of materials and possessions during my youth in the 1950s, we had more of a sense of community and order than is ever likely to be the case today.

My story represents in many ways a modern morality tale. I have lived life hard and certainly to the full and have always insisted on being 'top dog' whether in the business world or on the doors.

But I have discovered all too late that ultimately it means very little, compared to the joys of family life – that have been partly denied me – and being able to appreciate the finer points of our compromised world. I hope that, although this story is blunt and to the point, I have not offended any of those people I hold most dear.

I would like to think that for all my self-confessed wrong doings my wife Jackie understands me just a little bit more and my children and grandchildren will know that I love them and always will whether that be in this world or beyond.

To those who wish to open up their hearts in a similar way, I would say – don't take the decision lightly. It is a hard and a very personal thing to do and often you'll wonder whether the benefits will ever outweigh the heartaches.

But by learning about ourselves, perhaps we learn more about this strange old world.....